SHADO'
WESTE

Haunted Sites and Ancient
Mysteries of Upstate New York

BY MASON WINFIELD

LAURA WILDER

©1997 Western New York Wares Inc.
All rights reserved.
Printed by Petit Printing
First printing 1997
Second printing 1998
Third printing 1999

Address all inquires to:
Brian Meyer, Publisher
Western New York Wares Inc.
P.O. Box 733
Buffalo, NY 14205
(716)832-6088

This book was published in Buffalo, NY
ISBN: I-87920I-22-4

PUBLISHER'S PONDERINGS

Even as a kid, I was never afraid of ghosts, extra-terrestrials or other things that go bump in the night. My mom gets the credit for instilling in me a healthy curiosity about the paranormal. From an early age, she taught me and my three siblings that "spirits" are to be revered, not feared. I remember talking about the subject even at the tender age of five or six.

It came as no surprise to my father or the children when mom became a spiritualist in the 1970s. But Jean Meyer wasn't the stereotypical crystal ball-gazing cardboard cut-out that so many of us unfairly associate with spiritualism. Her beliefs are rooted in a deeply religious view that we are not alone as we stumble through life.

And so when a writer from East Aurora called my company to gauge our interest in publishing a book about paranormal happenings in Western New York, I was intrigued. More than intrigued. I was fascinated.

Mason Winfield has since become a respected and valued associate. Having worked with more than 20 authors over the past 13 years, I say without hesitation that Mason is among the most enthusiastic, hard-working and credible researchers to have ever hopped aboard the Western New York Wares bandwagon.

It's a privilege to put our publishing logo on this ground-breaking work. I only hope that our firm has the good fortune to collaborate with Mason on future literary ventures.

While I've never feared ghosts and goblins, the regional publishing business has "spooked me" on more than one occasion. The road to literary and financial success is paved with potholes, some of them the size of craters.

Someone once described publishing as "a marriage of art and business." Our unique company is hardly a one-man show. My profound thanks to Michele Ratzel who has spent six years making sure the financial end of the business isn't given short-shrift by the publisher's preoccupation with literary ventures.

Marketing Associate Matthew Pitts and his predecessor Kevin Wilson have played key roles in helping to make Western New York Wares Inc. the premier distributor of regional books.

John Hardiman of Petit Printing has been more than an "account executive." He has been a creative force in more than a dozen ventures, helping to shape the graphic elements and playing the role of watchdog in the tricky production process.

Finally, I thank my former wife, Pamela Cordaro Miles who co-founded a tiny mom-and-pop firm called Meyer Enterprises back in 1984. Her enthusiasm, creativity and hard work helped to lay the foundation for what is now Western New York Wares Inc. Pam instilled in me the confidence that I could accomplish some lofty goals if I worked hard enough and believed in myself.

With that, we hope you enjoy this journey down the fascinating path of the paranormal. Please write to us and let us know what you think!

Brian Meyer
September 1997

INTRODUCTION

For most of the twentieth century, it seems, Western New York has been on the short end of a pervasive geographic snobbery. The region's national image (symbolized in its nucleus, Buffalo) is probably that of a humble, rust-belt domain of faint initiative, withering spirits, and migrating talent - a homely place where not too much ever seems to happen. Some of this image problem is our own fault. A city that routes expressways through its Olmsted parks and between its citizenry and its waterfront cannot blame fate that its staple industry is not tourism. Even in spiritual senses the region seems out of public favor, as if no respectable vision-quest could skirt Taos or Stonehenge and conclude here. It was not always so.

The first White settlers of Western New York marveled at its relics and earthworks, evidence of earlier cultures whose settlement may have been more constant and populous than in any other region of the Americas. They stared into the ancient woods, across the landscape changing through its four full seasons, or down the peaceful creeks, and wondered mightily about their human history. By the middle of the nineteenth century this region seemed miraculous as a source of religious zeal that led to cults, communities (most of them countercultural), and two major modern religions. Many thought some occult energy native to the area must be behind this and its many other manifestations; this book - a paranormal survey of Western New York - is an informal consideration of just that subject.

Modern parapsychology - psychical (psi) research - has three general studies, almost all of which are conducted in laboratories:

◈ Extrasensory perception (ESP) in humans and animals
◈ Psychokinesis (PK, "mind over matter," "supernatural" physical abilities)
◈ "Theta" Research (life after death)

Despite this apparently clearcut chart, psychical research in the late 1990's seems to lack strong direction. Even as the AMA begins to consider alternate healing practices and computer printouts support the validity of astrology, the goals of psychical research societies are curiously diffuse, and elsewhere the defenders of psi research seem on the general run. However, the supernatural industry - that is, public interest in the subject for fun and guidance - is doing very well (as it usually does at the end of a century and does invariably at the end of a millennium).

This book is not psychical research. It is a regional survey into the "fuzzy fringe" (we'll use the term "paranormal" for almost all of it) that seems to flank the parameters of laboratory research: UFO's, mystery monsters, hauntings, earth energies, ancient anomalies, offbeat religious groups, magical societies, and even old-fashioned ghostlore. (Some of this, of course, with the fuzz off, represents real venues for understanding.) We ran the comb over Western New York and commented on some of what came up. The reader will find chapters in each of the rough categories that organized themselves as we went along.

We first got on to the idea of a book like this during research into Roycroft, East Aurora's Arts & Crafts Movement community which, we suspect, was involved with mysticism and maybe a bit more. Attempting to understand its location here, we dug into the roots of the region around it a little bit, and with each metaphoric spadeful, something else interesting came up. This, we figured, was a sign of something, and a story worth telling.

As we debated how to limit our survey area, we realized that probably any limit was artificial; if the paranormal disrespects earth's physical laws, it would hardly heed human geographical boundaries. The old Genesee Country, though, was New York State west of a line dropped south from Sodus Bay, along Seneca Lake through Elmira. This was the general territory of the Seneca Nation, the historic inhabitants of Western New York. Their old title was "The Keepers of the Western Door," the guardians of the western entrance to the landscape-longhouse their Iroquois Confederation was envisioned. Though they took this land from many others by force of arms, it was theirs when the Whites arrived, and we could not forget them in any page of our study of their traditional territory.

KENNETH SHERIDAN

DEDICATION:

for Mabel Z. Winfield
1896 - 1996

Und weil Grossmütterchen, das gute,
mir oft von Wünschegerten las
so traümte ich...

(Rilke)

You read to me of wishing-wands and so I dreamed.

CONTENTS

1. BURIED SECRETS
Ancient Mysteries ... 10

2. PLACES OF POWER
Supernatural Nature ... 30

3. TEN CLASSIC SPOOKS
19th Century Hauntings ... 46

4. THE SPIRIT WAY
The Trumpet of a Prophecy ... 68

5. THE STORYTELLER'S BAG
The Keepers of the Western Door ... 92

6. TRACK OF THE ILLUMINOIDS
The Secret Societies ... 114

Contents

7. The Supernatural Roycroft
East Aurora's Mystical Community ... 134

8. Ten Modern Spooks
20th-Century Hauntings ... 158

9. The Dragon Path
(With Franklin LaVoie)

FRANKLIN LAVOIE

BURIED SECRETS

Many of these can be seen
In quiet places, fields of green
Of hedgerowed lanes with countless names,
But the only thing that remains...

Steve Winwood, Jim Capaldi

ANCIENT MYSTERIES

Archaeological mysteries figure quite prominently in the late twentieth-century paranormal industry. We're so used to the idea that it no longer seems strange, but it probably should. There's nothing supernatural about ancient Europeans in America, for instance, or anthropoidal skulls in Western New York burial mounds. It's as if, though, to some paranormal students anything that flaunts one firmly-held theory of the world makes every other one fair game. Of interest to this chapter will be Western New York matters that seem to defy the orthodox picture of American prehistory, which (as of 1997) is roughly as follows:

◈ The Americas were peopled exclusively by anatomically modern humans - direct ancestors of today's Native Americans - from Asia before the end of the last Ice Age

◈ No ancestor of modern humankind ever lived in the Americas

◈ American cultures developed in isolation until Columbus arrived in 1492

So most archaeologists, historians, and anthropologists maintain. Yet evidence has been offered from all over the two American continents to suggest that there may have been at least some interchange of ideas, artifacts, or immigrants between the realms of Old World and New before Columbus. There are finds that even seem to indicate that a human ancestor - *Homo erectus*, perhaps - once lived in the Americas. At the least, this is thought-provoking.

As we write in the late 1990's the pace of progress of American archaeology is stunning. It's entirely possible that by the time this chapter is read its wildest surmises may appear basic. They may also be so convincingly refuted that we err for considering them at all. Ah well. Keep this caution in mind at all times: Beware of elaborate new theories when the old one has worked well for so long. That doesn't mean we should stop being curious.

MONSTERS FROM THE MOUND

[Some old historians dissed reports of bizarre finds from Western New York, but most acknowledged mystery. We should be suspicious of stories from frontier papers that stood to gain plenty from tall tales. These are from historical texts.]

When the Whites arrived, Western New York was littered with the works of earlier people. Stone walls, graded roads, and fortifications were reported, though most commonly these markers were earthen mounds or enclosures. The Native Americans seldom had any tradition about the people who had put them in place. Most of us now believe that the influence of the Mississippian (Mound-Builder) culture was behind them. The settlement and the plow have been lethal to most of these fragile works, and even the old mound-fanatic E. G. Squier confessed ruefully in 1849 that the Western Door held little any more worth looking at. As these works were destroyed in the last century a stablefull of curiosities seems to have come out.

T. Apoleon Cheney notes (in *Illustrations of the Ancient Monuments of Western New York*) that a twelve-foot high elliptical mound above Cattaraugus County's Conewango Valley held eight big human skeletons. Most crumbled, but a thigh bone was found to be 28" long. Exquisite stone points, enamelwork, and jewelry (like that of Mexico or Peru) were also unearthed in the area. The mound looked like those of the Old World.

Cheney also mentions a skeleton seven-foot-five (with an unusually thick skull) from a Chautauqua County site near Cassadaga Creek. Inside a very old mound near Cassadaga Lake were some large skeletons that were examined by "medical gentlemen." One measured nearly nine feet. (In 1938 Charles Hunnington of Randolph was so inspired by Doc Cheney's finds that he made two giant "wooden Indian" statues, probably still at the museum in Little Valley.)

The *History of Cattaraugus County* notes the town of Carrollton's "Fort Limestone," whose rough figure-eight enclosed five acres. In 1851 the removal of a stump turned up a mass of human bones. Some were enormous. Franklinville's Marvin Older virtually gamboled about the site with them: a skull fit over his size seven-and-a-half head; a rib curved all the way around him, a shinbone went from his ankle to above his knee, and a jaw - with bodacious molars - went over his own. Its first owner had probably stood eight feet tall.

Stafford Cleveland's *History and Directory of Yates County* refers to skeletons from a conical burial mound by Keuka Lake in the early 1800's. A Penn Yan doctor found that many were seven footers. (Tales of ghosts and buried treasure cling to this vicinity as well.)

Turner's *History of the Holland Purchase* reports an ancient three-acre earth fort in Orleans county (about one and a half miles west of Shelby Center) that covered seven - and eight-foot skeletons. Their skulls were well developed in front, broad between the ears, and flattened on top.

Also, Turner notes that, upon digging a cellar on his town of Aurora farm, Charles P. Pierson found a giant of his own.

The 1879 *History of Allegany County* noted a circular mound between Philip's Creek and the Genesee in the village of Belmont. Several feet high and fifteen or so in diameter, it disgorged human bones, some very large, when the railroad was made in 1849 and 1850.

Giant human skeletons don't ring any bells with us. Some think the Scandinavians were in Western New York, and they were considered virtual giants in the ancient world (whose people were traditionally much shorter than those now). Many Vikings would seem tall even today, but they were not routinely seven-footers.

Not all the humanlike skeletons found about the Western Door were so surely human. Several old histories discuss the two very bizarre skulls taken in the early 1820's from a mound on Tonawanda Island near Buffalo. One early writer notes each "portentous, protruding lower jaw and canine forehead." Another adds that the burial customs were entirely unlike those of the region's natives.

Our County and Its People (Truman C. White, 1898) mentions skeletons that seem to have been "platycnemic" - flat-shinned. In the bluff at Fort Porter (Buffalo) one such skeleton was found near ancient implements. Burials of up to three such skeletons have been found high up on river or lake banks about the region. Their flat shins and "other skeletal peculiarities" were thought due to climbing and living in trees. These are odd stories to make up.

In nature's evident experiments toward Homo sapiens, some of the discontinued models were very large (*Gigantopithecus* comes to mind); none are thought to have set foot or dragged knuckle on any American soil. Jess Stearn (in *Montezuma's Serpent*) cites finds from the American southwest implying some giant, bestial hominid was here. Jim Brandon's *Weird America* lists two such accounts from just outside the Western Door. An eight-footer turned up in an Ellisburg, PA mound (near Wellsville, NY) in 1886. The same year a team of professors and professionals found dozens of huge, oddly-skulled humans in a mound in Sayre, PA (near Elmira, NY). They averaged seven feet, though some were taller, and some had horny knobs on their foreheads. Several went to the American Investigating Museum in Philadelphia, into which they disappeared. Modern fans of Bigfoot (seen in almost all the states of the Union) might rejoice at historical testimony of monster bones; for the rest of us the matter is just...weird.

BLUFF POINT

["The strangest work known in anthropology," wrote Dr. Samuel H. Wright in 1898 of this Yates County site near Penn Yan. Most of our information comes from interviews with Yates County historians.]

The region's seen a lot of history, not all of it peaceable. During the Revolution on Sullivan's campaign a lot of White guys from other parts of the colonies got a look at the western Finger Lakes. After the Revolution, parcels of land were handed out to veterans, and many chose theirs back here.

Not all the history here is the comfortable kind, either, that fits neatly into existing categories. A group of anomalous artifacts have been found about the general region north and west of Keuka Lake. The biggest mystery of all was Bluff Point.

Keuka Lake is a big natural Y with its fork to the north. At the base of the promontory that runs into the middle of the lake, on a line drawn between the Y's top stems, is Bluff Point. Eight hundred feet over the lake, Bluff Point is a splendid overlook of the surrounding territory whose summit was once the site of a strange construction of tooled stone. Large rectangular blocks resembling ramparts, even the foundations of a big building, had been arranged and left for posterity's befuddlement. When the early settlers asked the Native Americans who put it there, "Your guess is as good as ours" was the essence of their reply. It may be that way today.

Bluff Point was not a fort; no natural spring was in the middle of it, a vital factor in withstanding a siege. It was probably a ceremonial site, because of both its vantage and the parallel walkways, eight feet wide, once there. (They might have had astronomical alignment.) The Native Americans of the Northeast Woodlands didn't build like this, as far as we know.

Reporter and amateur archaeologist Gil Brewer did a lot of digging at Bluff Point in the first half of the twentieth century. Widely remembered for his patience with the many youngsters who helped on his projects, Brewer found a beautifully-worked copper projectile point and artifacts in bits and pieces with traces of enameling on them. The image on a worked stone looked to Brewer like a veiled woman, though not everyone saw it. Brewer later left the area, and his collection of artifacts has been hard to trace. Now there are only newspaper accounts of what he found.

Brewer never came up with a firm theory about the Bluff Point stoneworks. At various times he thought Vikings and even Assyrians (which seems a bigger stretch) might be behind them. Neither the site nor the drawings of it struck chords in those who saw them, but every-one agreed Bluff Point was very strange.

Without seeing the Bluff Point ruins, it's hard to have any firm opinion. Modern studies of the site were never made. Carbon-dating will never reveal when the stones were put in place, nor will surveying and other study tell us if they had astronomical purpose or positioning relative to other sites in the region. Like too many of America's treasures and curiosities, this one no longer exists. "The Stoneworks" on Bluff Point were dismantled in the middle of the twentieth century. Today, they survive only in the foundations of the Wagner Mansion (at the south of the point where, allegedly, most of the stone went), and in some drawings made around the 1930's. We bitterly lament the destruction of history, and possibly more, the destruction of all chance to settle historical mystery.

THE ALLEGANY SLAUGHTER-STONE

[Like UFOs, unlikely historic objects ("UHOs") are often reported in flurries. Western New York has its own contributions, and two come from the Allegany hills.]

For years the large piece of sandstone had been in open view in an Allegany State Park playground. No one had made much of it until 1976, when someone noticed among its markings what appeared to be writing.

Public interest in "UHOs" was then at a high. *America, B. C.* (by Harvard's Barry Fell) was in the throes of the sensation it caused, claiming to prove that Old World traders and explorers had been to the American continents long before Columbus' 1492 arrival. This book set hordes of professionals and amateurs scurrying about the hills, fields, valleys, and rivers of our nation for other traces. The Allegany stone came to Fell's attention.

Late New Zealander H. Barraclough Fell (whom we were privileged to have known) was the patron saint of the modern study of ancient cross-Atlantic contact. He was an oceanographer and a linguist, a professor of biology at Harvard, but also a world-renowned epigrapher - a translator of ancient inscriptions. To one of the park's old hands, the markings on the Allegany stone looked like "worm crawlings," but to Fell it was an authentic artifact. He cautioned that it was severely frost-damaged, and that most of the letters had to be reconstructed. Nevertheless, he deciphered some words of a Celtic-Iberian language written in a type of Arabic script called "pre-Classic." With some adjustment (such as the addition of vowels, commonly absent in rock inscriptions), Fell determined that this was more or less the tombstone of a certain "King Zari."

Paul R. Huey (then senior scientist in archaeology for the New York State Parks) seemed uninspired by the Allegany stone, commenting that any significant European presence in this part of America would have left "evidence of their impact on native culture." Barry Fell countered that there was plenty already.

Fell cited "Mystery Hill," a complex of megalithic-style stone structures near Salem, NH (which appear to have astronomical alignments and Celtic inscriptions); the mysterious Davenport calendar stone, inscribed with astronomical ideas in three ancient languages [Egyptian, Iberian Punic (Phoenician), and Libyan], found deep in a Native American burial mound in Iowa; the apparent incorporation of Egyptian hieroglyphics into the (Canadian) Micmac language and writing; and many other cases, including ancient, European-style, hard-metal artifacts.

After its day in the sun the Allegany stone was kept in a warehouse. A mid-80's fire in this building almost totally destroyed the soft sandstone. Photographs, and even a video about the stone, survive. Fell's identification of its writing was not as farfetched as it might seem. Many Mediterranean peoples were fine sailors. Their crews would have-been mixed populations and their written language likely that of the nearest large, literate culture. Other evidence of contact from the ancient Iberian Peninsula (Spain) has turned up about Western New York, which does lie on common routes of in-continent water travel.

Obviously, we shouldn't go too far to interpret marks on rocks. With enough tinkering, something can be made of almost any set of scratches. (Erik Von Daniken's *Chariots of the Gods* fan club is notorious for novel reconstructions of ancient imagery on walls and pots. All it takes to correct those impressions is one discussion with a responsible scholar.) There are good cases of old European writing found in the Americas, even in the Western Door; we're not sure the Allegany stone is among them.

But that's not all for the region. Another mysterious stone found on a ridge nearby was displayed at a ceremony in Salamanca in the 1930's. This artifact is a large flat stone with runnels at the sides, an apparent slaughter-stone much like those of Central America. The Senecas claimed it was the sacrificial stone of a tribe that had been there well before them. If this is the case, it's a rare one; while human sacrifice was endemic to parts of Central and South America, it was all but nonexistent in the Northeast Woodlands. This stone might be the sign of a cultural influence totally unfamiliar to the historians. .

Park historians have been tracking this tale down for a while now, and still the only source is a single seventy-year-old newspaper report. This is suspicious. A large flat-topped rock of similar description was once called "a corn-grinding stone" by park tour guides, but some Seneca laugh at that. "That was where we made our weapons," said one of them, still proud of his martial ancestors, implying that the troughs on the stone were for straightening spear and arrow shafts, and its other furrows for sharpening flint points. Until more definitive evidence turns up, the story of the slaughter-stone seems unreliable. One of the biggest jokes in the Longhouse has always been to leave gullible Whites (who had not inquired with the proper manners) dangling in a misconception.

THE CHAUTAUQUA VIKINGS

[In 1898 the famous and controversial "Kensington Runestone" was found in Minnesota. A message of exploration, desperation, and death seems to be written in an old Germanic script (not exactly like those in the texts). An eleventh-century Norse coin - apparently found at an archaeological site in Maine - and the Newport, RI stone tower are also puzzling objects. Western New York may have its own contributions to the "Vikings-were-here" contest.]

For many years Eber Russell (1881-1968) was the Town of Perrysburg Historian. The lore of the Iroquois was one of the great interests of his long life, and it may have pointed him to another. Old Native American legends and unusual artifacts in his own region led Russell to believe that, well before Columbus, someone from a long way away had explored North America and even passed through his own Chautauqua County. Russell came to believe it was the medieval Norse, that these seafarers had a trail connecting the Mohawk River or Lake Ontario with the "metalliferous regions" around the upper Great Lakes - probably for trade in copper - and that they had left some unmistakable markers. (Someone surely was mining enormous quantities of copper near Lake Superior thousands of years ago, way before the Viking era.)

Old Norse sagas talk of discoveries and colonies in new lands that certainly could have been the Americas. Many scholars believe the Norse explored the New World, and offer evidence placing them along the Atlantic coasts and in inland areas of the North American continent between the ninth and the fourteenth centuries. Several apparently Norse relics, many of them bronze and iron, have been found in the Great Lakes region, perhaps a center of Norse activity.

His theory of "the Chautauqua Vikings" was Eber Russell's pet. His evidence:

🌼 Metal ax marks dating to Medieval times found in the 1830's in an oak tree at Lyons, Wayne County. (Marks like these were also found near East Aurora, Erie County. Tree-ring evidence dated them before Columbus.)

🌼 The Sodus Bay spearhead, now in the Wayne County Museum. (Found in 1929, this apparently European artifact is one of a handful from the Great Lakes.)

🌼 Two stone axes. (What makes these Norse?)

🌼 An iron kettle full of flint arrow points found in a Native American mound near Quaker Bridge about 1900. (Russell figured the kettle had to be Norse because only their iron was pure enough to withstand the elements that long.)

🌼 A stone face from Conewango Swamp that "looked Norse."

🌼 A "Danish stone" (of some sort) mentioned in the Little Valley paper.

"Norse holes" near East Aurora and about Chautauqua County. (These mystifying "mooring stones" get their treatment later.)

 Old Seneca legends (and Eber Russell's deductions from them):
  - a Viking-style boat found in Pymatuning Swamp
  - "a great canoe with flowing-haired men and shiny shields on Lake Ontario"
  - a ship prow found near Sodus Bay

 Swords and five winged copper Norse helmets from Ohio mounds.

 Remnants of an apparent pre-Columbian European-style campsite on a Chautauqua County farm. On a nearby slope is a Z-shaped mound under which Russell found the remains of a wall.

Truman White mentions two brass kettles found beneath the city of Buffalo in the late 1800's. Between them and the surface were three or four feet of earth and layers of Native American artifacts. They were taken by many to be evidence of some earlier-than-expected European contact, probably Viking.

Barry Fell (*Saga America*) believed Iroquois shells (used as currency) were quite similar to "crosscut" coins given by the Dark Ages Anglo-Saxons as part of the "Danegeld" (their tribute to Danish kings), and likely evidence of Viking contact. In 1962 Frederick Pohl (who wrote books on Viking explorations of America) examined Russell's supposed Norse settlement at Mud Lake. He seemed unimpressed with the "Nordicity" of the site, even suggesting that it looked more like the left-overs of Celtic habitation. A small "rune stone" found near the site and a still smaller one from Ellington in the Little Valley museum appeared to Pohl closer to Celtic ogham or Middle Eastern cuneiform than they did to runes. He was more curious about the eight-foot skeletons reportedly found nearby. (See "Monsters from the Mound.")

Ancient Europeans might have made it across the Atlantic to the Americas, and Scandinavian Vikings would be good candidates. Their navigating skills and settling inclinations are well demonstrated in Greenland, halfway across the Atlantic. Russell's evidence may indicate a visit by some folks from the Old World to Chautauqua County, but nothing we see so far proves it was the Norse.

EPHRAIM WOODRUFF'S BURIED TABLET

East Aurora's first Euroamerican resident was a blacksmith-farmer named Ephraim Woodruff. He had his tract in the southwest side of the town, probably on Prospect Avenue near what's now the West Oakwood Cemetery. His own stone is in its eastern cousin, half a mile up the same street, behind the Spiritualist Temple.

In 1807 the plow turned up something unusual in Woodruff's field. A footnote near the end of Turner's *History of the Holland Purchase* tells us most of what we know about this object, an eight by ten inch rectangular tablet about a quarter of an inch thick. Smith Woodruff would have known immediately that it was made of copper. One side was inscribed with illegible writing, and the other with an architectural image.

Sometime before the 1830's the practical blacksmith hammered the soft copper into dining utensils, a ladle and skimmer upon which (according to Turner) some of the markings were still clear. By the 1840's Woodruff's offspring had moved, taking skimmer and ladle with them. Later generations may have made it to California, where descendants of the stolid blacksmith may still reside.

Sometime in the 1840's some professors from the University of Buffalo quizzed the locals who had seen Woodruff's odd plate. No firm impression of the script on it could be formed from the recollections of these folk (who spent little enough time with letters in their own language). We can deduce that the characters were so non-representational that they could hardly have been hieroglyphics (picture-writing). More likely they were phonetic characters (representing sounds) like those of our own alphabet. They were described as resembling old-time musical notes, which reminds some observers of Celtic ogham writing.

This is a curiosity. Though the sophisticated cultures of Central and South America certainly had means of non-spoken communication, at Columbus' arrival the Aztecs were probably the only Native American society that could read and write. Neither American continent had phonetic writing. Maybe the closest to it was the intricate Maya system of blended glyphs and sounds. However, Mayan script would be hard to mistake for an alphabet, and the Yucatan is a long way from Prospect Avenue. Woodruff's plate was found near a navigable stream, a few hours' canoe cruise from Lake Erie.

The image on the other side was another oddity. The UB professors had brought illustrated books about many ancient cultures to East Aurora. Among these was one by American diplomat John Lloyd Stevens and British artist Frederick Catherwood about their travels throughout Central America. Catherwood's sublime illustrations of Mayan ruins amid jungle settings spellbound the middle-of-the-nineteenth-century world. It was one of the images (stepped pyramid, ornamented wall, inscribed stone) in this book that struck a chord with the early East Aurorans who had seen Ephraim Woodruff's plate.

It should be pointed out that quirky inscriptions may present a bigger problem than first appears. While an incomprehensible piece of chiseling found about the American northeast might easily be written off as a recent fake, Jim Brandon (*The Rebirth of Pan*) points out not only that bizarre inscriptions are also found about the Old World, but that many of them seem to share symbols with the ones found in the New. It is almost as if there may be one and perhaps even several ancient codes at work. What may be behind it is the problem.

A word or two about copper. Use of the metal alone does not imply an influence from outside the American continents. Many Native American societies used copper, though they didn't smelt it, and its use was largely ornamental. We have alluded to the copper-mining in the upper Great Lakes regions that may have begun five thousand years ago. (Somebody was interested in very large amounts of copper; we don't know who, or where it all went, and the Native Americans had no ideas.) A metallurgist reminds us that copper might decompose very rapidly in soil of one type; in that near where Woodruff's plate was found, it could last quite a long time. This artifact could have been very old.

Aurora antiquarian Rodger Sweetland likes to conjecture that in some old family chest in the villages south of Buffalo, or in an Ohio, Kansas, or California town along the likely route of the Woodruff family, some tracing of the blacksmith's plate may turn up, maybe the original implements made from it. A glance at either would speak volumes.

THE GENESEE TRADE-TOKEN

Sometime in the mid-1970's, the late William Johnson found a curious stone in the stream bed of the Genesee River, near the Allegany County village of Belfast. This small, hard, oval tablet bears some of the clearest ancient European-style markings ever found in either American continent. Even to the dilettante they look like characters in a Mediterranean-style alphabet.

William Johnson, Sr., was a Belfast native and an avid hunter of Native American relics. He seemed to regard this find as a curiosity and no more; but upon his return from military service in the late 1970's, Bill Johnson, Jr., set about getting an answer. Harvard's Barry Fell believed he had it.

The late Professor Fell thought the neat markings on the Genesee stone were in "the South Iberic alphabet" from ancient Spain. Their language is "Arabic-related Iberic," the business language of southern Spain centuries before Columbus. So far, so good. How did it get to the banks of the Genesee?

To Fell, this was a trading token, one of the best examples of Iberic script ever seen here. (With some laboring, he translated the characters into something like, "Confirmation: I have pledged to pay in full.") Other inscriptions from northeastern states (for example, our own Allegany script-stone) seem to be in a similar lingo. Artifacts like these caused Fell and others to believe that there was ancient commerce between Old World and New, possibly trade in animal pelts and copper.

We hear the Genesee stone was shown to Fell about a month too late to make it into *America, B. C.* Nevertheless, his theory was in full flight. Like so many other supposed ancient European artifacts in North America, this stone was found near a navigable waterway. The Genesee River is in the St. Lawrence water shed, emptying into Lake Ontario near Rochester.

It's just about impossible to date a stone artifact that was found in isolation, but you can get clues. The edges of the characters on the Genesee stone have been carefully examined with a stereo microscope; they were cut a long time ago.

In her memoirs, Mary Jemison (1743-1833, the famous "White Woman of the Genesee") recalled an oddity. A heavy rain had once washed strange human skeletons out of the bank of Fall Brook near a bend in the Genesee River. The Seneca had no explanations, but were sure these were not the remains of Native Americans. Other old Seneca legends concern a strange Canisteo community, "outlandish" in dress and appearance. Many think these were Europeans.

Sometimes the venerable Professor Fell (a world-famous scholar) deciphered writing on boulders where this book's author (a country English teacher) could see only asymmetrical scratches. The Genesee stone is not among them. It appears to be an ancient European artifact. It could, of course, have been smuggled over in recent times and simply dropped in its new location. We doubt it. It seems to add to the evidence that the picture of ancient America is not so tidy as once it seemed.

THE MYSTERIOUS MOORING STONES

A handful of weighty stones with odd holes in them have been found about the Western Door. The size and material vary from stone to stone, but the holes are uncannily precise: narrow (about one inch), deep (up to eight inches), and of a strange shape (referred to as "lobed-triangular" - an equilateral triangle with curved sides). Just why Eber Russell thought the Vikings made these stones is a mystery to us.

Holed stones like these - from northern Europe, New England, and the Great Lakes - are usually found near lakes, seacoasts, and navigable streams, so some think they were used to anchor boats. A line attached to a stick thrust into the hole should have done the job. Their prevalence north of the Equator meant they must have been devised by some adventurous European nautical people.

Russell noted the rectangular shape and compass alignment of one of the Chautauqua County "mooring stones," and declared it similar to the controversial "Kensington Runestone." On August 2, 1959, with about twenty people present (including a geologist, a reporter, a civil engineer, and Judge Lee Towne Adams), the stone was overturned by tractors to reveal the hidden side. Russell claimed to see letters graven there. Some people were impressed by the characters, some saw none at all. At best the inscriptions (which Russell traced) were crude, and, after a month of exposure, they flaked away.

Many anti-Viking theorists point out with faintly muffled gloating that none of these old stones are identifiably Scandinavian artifacts. Yet the chuckles disappear when they are asked to explain what Native American culture might have made them, and others would like to see these perfect holes made at all.

We've seen modern, natural reduplications of some mind-boggling stonework that had been claimed as evidence of ancient high-tech. Our "mooring holes" - so narrow, deep, and smooth - may be different. In the 1950's Frederick Pohl (eager to prove Vikings were here) made a one-inch hole in granite using a steel chisel, and claimed the screwy lobed-triangular shape was a natural result of the process. He does not claim, though, that his hole came out uncannily smooth. There's little doubt that the stones about the Western Door are old, and they would have been little use to the known historic explorers of the region. At the very least they seem to point - if not to ancient astronauts - to some unexpected visitors to the area.

IROQUOIS CELTS

Though in many minds the Celts will always be associated with Ireland (one of the last holdouts of Celtic culture), they were the first historic people of northern Europe, inhabiting most of the continent at some point in history. They may even have settled and explored North America. A surprisingly good case can be made for Prince Madoc of Wales, who, according to some, colonized North America in 1170. Irish monks may have preceded Madoc by a few centuries, and well before the time of Christ full-scale Celtic migrations may have come from Spain.

A batch of old stories feature White settlers encountering Native American speakers of Irish or Welsh Celtic languages. Mysterious stone ruins - widely found throughout New England and New York, suspiciously similar to ones in the Old World - are also used to advance the theory of ancient Celtic influence. It's been suggested that the Iroquois were influenced by Celtic contact, possibly even that the groups intermarried. We can discuss some similarities between Iroquois culture and the old Celts we know best, those of the British Isles.

Though Barry Fell thought he found connections between Celtic and Algonquin root words, we doubt that any true linguistic links between Iroquois and Celt would have hidden this long. There are some similarities in lore, however. Shape-shifting was a prime power of both Celtic and Iroquois wizards, and "The Little People" make one of the most interesting matches between the cultures. The Celts had many tribes and echelons among their fairy folk, some of whom are small. (The Iroquois Little People are discussed in our chapter "The Storyteller's Bag.") In both cultures, the Little People are identified with natural forces, and can become small animals (birds or bugs) and spy on humans. They have many magical arts and objects, though they need human help for some unlikely things. Time often passes supernaturally in their presence.

The Iroquois game of lacrosse, though widely played in the northeast and likely not an Iroquois invention, is a bit like hurling, the inveterate game of the Irish Celts. Both sports involve fields, teams, sticks, and balls, and are merely indirect versions of armed combat.

The Iroquois, the People of the Longhouse, indeed had a central structure quite critical to their social organization, similar to the "meadhall" found all over iron-age Europe and spoken of in the Saxon epic *Beowulf*. The Iroquois seem to have had many temperamental similarities with the old Celts as we know them. Both groups were warlike and almost superhumanly courageous, though not terribly disciplined when it came to open-field army-fighting. Both cultures prized poetry and oratory, and lived in similar societal organizations. Had it ever occurred to a Celt, however, to form a union (like the Iroquois confederacy) with his or her cultural cousins, Europe would be a far different place today.

The Iroquois are matrilineal, meaning they trace their descent through the mother. Some Celtic groups, though not all, were among northern Europe's last matrilineal cultures. Women have major roles and close to full equality in Iroquois society, much like they did in the old Celtic and Germanic cultures as described by the Romans. (Joseph Campbell believed northern Europe's misogynistic tendencies were Mediterranean imports.)

There are surely suggestions that the Celts may have been about the Western Door. T. Apoleon Cheney (*Illustrations of the Ancient Monuments of Western New York*) depicts a sandstone head that looks not at all Native American (though he suspected it was Toltec or Aztec). It looks like some famous Celtic heads found in Europe. Barry Fell (*Saga America*) believed Iroquois artifacts like combs and carved shells closely resembled Celtic combs and Saxon coins (from a time when Celt and Saxon were in close contact). In his search for Vikings Frederick Pohl examined sites and artifacts in Chautauqua County and believed them all more Celtic than anything. Whether Celt and Iroquois influenced each other is another question.

Cultural similarities as general as the ones we have mentioned do not prove contact, and there seems no need to look overseas for parallels. Other Native American groups show features the Iroquois share with the Celts. We suspect that, had there been significant European presence in the Americas, Native American ideas would have been more similar to those of the Old World, and that at least a few American things would have made their way back across the Atlantic. (Europe could certainly have used corn and potatoes a long time before it got them.) If Iroquois met Celt, it was a dead-end on this continent, for nothing we know of Iroquois made its way back. The best support for the idea of contact between the groups would be evidence - archaeological, linguistic, or genetic - which seems not yet to exist.

VALLEY OF THE LOST NATION

Allegany County's North Valley is the hilly, wooded realm of hunting and outdoor sports. North of Centerville and south of Eagle and Bliss, it once was home to a talented Amerindian tribe so completely vanished from history that it's known only as "The Lost Nation." The story should be located in time.

Well before the Whites had settled the interior of the continent, hot war had raged for much of the seventeenth-century, spilling blood as far east as the Hudson River and as far west as Lake Huron, spilling past the Great Smokies in the south, and, in the north, Lakes Erie and Ontario. The Iroquois Confederacy was on its crusade to control the southern Great Lakes, and therefore, the fur trade and all the wealth and power that came with it. By 1700 the then-Five Nations had cleared New York, Pennsylvania, and Ohio of all rivals. No power native to either American continent could have broken their hold.

History holds no fiercer fighter than the Iroquois. Some call their struggle with their Huron and Algonquin neighbors "the deadliest Indian civil war of all time." While the wars of Central and South America must surely have involved more combatants and equivalent ferocity, this woodland conflict was dire enough for those caught between its mighty opposites, as may have been the Lost Nation.

From the traces of them that survive, we can deduce that the Lost Nation was industrious, possibly praised by their neighbors for their crafts. But no one knows their language, their culture, their identity, or their fate. They just vanished.

Some "lowest-common denominators" can be offered. Had the Lost Nation been an Iroquois ally, it would have been protected; as a neutral nation, its people might flee battles, but still return; as an enemy, it would have been expunged in a single stroke evident to archaeology. From there, we run out of inference. Whatever the fate of this mystery tribe, they had gone to it by the end of the eighteenth century. The 1794 Canandaigua treaty named tribes and territories in the Western Door, but none that could be the Lost Nation.

Some think the Lost Nation was a group of Pequots such as had come to the Finger Lakes from Connecticut, migrated again, and vanished. Old Seneca lore may suggest that the Lost Nation was the Tudulo tribe, of whom nothing but the name is left. The trouble is that there's no evidence; evidence is always nice. Barring some we probably will never have, the Lost Nation they remain. We think of Richard Wilbur's sublime lyric, "To the Etruscan Poets" whose very language was lost: "Dream fluently, still brothers..." Just so.

WHITE INDIANS

["I've got a White guy with a stone point in him," proclaimed anthropologist James Chatters in the 1996 *New York Times*. When a Caucasian skeleton was found near Kennewick, Washington, with a flint shard embedded in its pelvic bone, Chatters and others thought they had a nineteenth-century settler, till the skeleton turned out to be 8500 years old. The skull, limbs, and teeth of the Kennewick man are typical of Caucasians, and independent studies of the remains turn up "White guy" every time. What he was doing in America eight thousand years before Columbus is anybody's guess.

DNA material in Kennewick man's bones should clarify the matter - if further study is allowed. A Native American group near the site is insisting upon "repatriating" (burying) the remains, refusing even to allow study as the matter is litigated. We hope they will not stand in the way of knowledge. Even if the Kennewick matter never clears itself, it's a clear example of how risky it is to write about prehistoric America in the late 1990's. So much is changing so fast.]

There is evidence that some ancient people settled places we never thought they visited, clearly complicating the modern picture of the ancient world. (We refer to the by-now well-known mummies, clearly North European types, in China - some of them four thousand years old.) It's not so neat and certain who lived where when. The same mystery may hold to this continent. Many Native American cultures have old legends of European-like people in several motifs:

❀ Individuals or single families of light-skinned people. Apparently genetic freaks, they live in native tribes.

❀ Whole tribes of Whites, usually hostile to their Native American neighbors, not too different in culture or lifestyle.

❀ White teacher-kings along the Maya/Aztec/Inca model. Legendary figures Kukulkan, Quetzalcoatl, and Viracocha were so prominent and so similar that most historians believe there must be some basis in fact. Each figure comes in a boat, gives laws and learning, then departs.

The archaeological evidence of ancient Europeans in the Americas is often far from firm, but it's led to a two-centuries-old myth-industry, also in motifs:

❀ Early explorers. This is the theme of an undocumented migration or settlement by historic peoples everyone agrees exists - Vikings, for instance, or Phoenicians. Only their presence in the Americas is problematic.

❀ The Mormon model of Lost Civilizations. This has a religious frame-work. The only source of proof is revelation, and all Native Americans are presumed sprung from the lost tribes of Israel. Some Mormon and Masonic nineteenth-century writers went to great lengths to develop this theory.

◈ Tribes of White Indians encountered by European/American explorers in remote regions of South and Central America. This is almost an early twentieth-century "Explorers' Club" folktale.

◈ Tribes of White Indians encountered by European/American settlers in North America. These are often downtrodden descendants of Welsh, Irish, or other European immigrants who made it over the Atlantic not too long before Columbus.

◈ Secret Societies. Some suspect that the medieval Templars maintained contact with the New World, hiding or accumulating treasure here.

Western New York makes its own contributions to the lore. According to W. W. Canfield's *Legends of the Iroquois*, the Seneca warrior and storyteller Cornplanter related ancient tales of White people. In some, these exceptional folk were obviously freaks, members of a single family. Cornplanter also tells tales of White settlers on the southern shores of the Great Lakes, long before the French or English. They were driven out of the region centuries before Cornplanter's time by native tribes coming down from Canada. (According to some, the Modena map Columbus used held evidence of a European colony on Lake Ontario.)

In *The Towpath* Arch Merrill points out another Western New York connection. Brockport explorer Richard March encountered tribes of Whites in the jungles of Panama. He brought some individuals back to the outer world in 1924. Their light hair and skin caused a stir till they were labeled "albinos" and the matter left in its simplest form. The historians we've interviewed don't seem to know much about explorer March, and we wonder what there is to the story.

The one up-side of the complete burning of the rain forest, which continues apace as we write in the late 1990's, is that it should leave nowhere to hide for lost cities, fabulous beasts, mysterious tribes, or any other jungle mysteries, including any "White Indians" who may ever have existed. It's doubtful, however, that at that point of eco-collapse the rest of humanity will be very interested. We will all be too busy looking after our own skins - those of us that are left - to worry about the color of anyone else's.

PLACES OF POWER

JEFF MILLER

Once again we have to face the frustrating recognition that no theory of the paranormal seems to be able to accommodate all the facts.
Colin Wilson

SUPERNATURAL NATURE

Some branches of the loose study we call the paranormal are devoted to the energies of the earth. According to ancient mysticism and modern instruments, some places just have more juice, and supernatural lore seems to gather about them. Here we study natural sites about the Western Door that have supernatural reputations. That seems straight-forward enough; but some readers may be surprised that we have included other things (like UFOs) that might seem to be anything but natural. There may be a connection.

In the 1960's British researcher John Michell began his career searching for the truth about UFOs. Two decades of worldwide study had not yet confirmed their existence, but the phenomenon was not without its patterns. UFOs were so often reported about old religious sites ("places of ancient sanctity") that Michell became more interested in the sites them-selves. He and others came to suspect that these were special spots in the earth, and that, somehow, the UFO matter was related.

Other patterns involved UFO "zones" about the world, two of them in the Western Door. Curious beastie sightings (Bigfoot, lake serpents, ghosts) seem to be part of the matter. (The third week of May 1977 found the British Isles a supernatural circus of "big cat" and Nessie sightings with a veritable "Star Wars" bigtop of UFOs above.) Both the Western Door zones are prominent in Native American mystical-religious lore and known for beastie sightings.

It developed that natural phenomena (like solar flares) were also implicated in the UFO mess. Even the dates are suspicious. The traditional beginning of the UFO craze in America was June 24, 1947 - St. John's Day, a heavy fest to the secret societies and near enough Midsummer's Day to be it. Even mythic patterns were replayed: the most commonly reported visual phenomena (bright discs, big serpents, big monkeys) are all simple, primal images of Jungian significance, such likely things to be imagined that we must pause and wonder. Of course, there could always be another explanation for many people reporting the same thing at the same time: that it was there.

There is some rare, good evidence in the UFO-beastie mess that seems to stand out from all the whoppers, and at least causes us to survey the matter. There could be sensible reasons that mystery remains. Many remote bogie-haunts have never been satisfactorily explored, and natural animals can go "undiscovered" for a long time. As for UFOs, well, if their builders are slick enough to cross galaxies we would expect them to outwit forever the species that supports disco.

THE GREAT LAKES TRIANGLE

[In the 1970's Charles Berlitz' observations made famous "the Bermuda Triangle," a tract of Atlantic water between Miami, Bermuda, and Puerto Rico. An even more impressive pattern of disaster may hedge the Western Door.]

So many ships and planes have vanished into a patch of ocean off the coast of Florida that "The Bermuda Triangle" is by now proverbial. We've seen conjecture that the tragic pattern is not out of measure with the size and traffic of the area, but that's not good enough for everyone, and there are many theories. Natural but as yet misunderstood effects could be at work. Geomagnetic disturbances may down planes by confounding their instruments. Rare, isolated, violent weather effects might finish them the old-fashioned way. "Earth burps" (gigantic gas bubbles from the ocean floor) could swamp ships. Ivan Sanderson popularized the theory of "vile vortices," regions on his "Earth-Grid" map of the globe where catastrophes flourish. Some people make the UFO connection; to them the disappearances are abductions, accidents, or even assaults. Others find the nearby "Bimini Wall" (a huge underwater formation of cyclopean blocks) a road to Atlantis, the ancient super-culture whose submerged high-tech outposts may still disrupt shipping and flight.

The Great Lakes may have their own trilateral of doom. Jay Gourley notes a panorama of air and water disaster about the five huge inland bodies in the two centuries they have been widely traveled. His 1977 book *The Great Lakes Triangle* notes a host of bizarre circumstances that seem to be part of an unholy pattern.

Doom falls with amazing speed and curious details. Sudden irrational behavior on the part of airmen and sailors (in many cases the sole cause of disaster) is widely reported. Pilots fail to switch from one fuel tank to another, crashing a plane by running out of gas. They talk casually as they drop into earth or lake, when every instrument in the cockpit should have been blaring, and a glance out a window would have given the alarm. Some scream and moan in panic, seemingly hurled in a roller-coaster of disorientation, unsure even of the direction of gravity. Co-pilots often watch calmly as another slides them into a forest or kamikazes into a runway. Skydivers, too, make suicidal moves, unhooking good chutes and failing to open reserves. It's as if some force is at work affecting the fabric of distance, direction, and time, and confounding human sensibilities.

Memory loss, particularly among survivors of air disasters, is remarkable. These people are questioned closely by investigators, and usually have no recollection of any aspect of their journey, certainly not the circumstances of the accident. Telepathic experiences - in both victims and their families - seem at a high. Then there are the disappearances without trace in heavily traveled waters. Pilots carry on conversations with airports after they have vanished from radar, before they vanish forever. Ships, even huge lake freighters, seem to drop with supernatural suddenness, as if the hand of a god had plucked them under.

They make the UFO connection to the Great Lakes Triangle as well. Many pilots report being tracked by nocturnal lights. Their instruments go wild, and their cockpits overheat insufferably if they come too close to the strange craft.

Part of the confusion relates to the disposition of the bodies after disasters. Some amazing things have been recorded. Victims of one shipwreck are found wearing life preservers from another, far away. One body turned out to be such an exact double of a man - down to scars, tattoos, and birthmarks - that his family identified it as him. Then the real man turned up, a survivor. In other cases, bodies are simply missing from closed cockpits of dashed planes.

In Charles Berlitz' search to explain the Bermuda Triangle, one of the more famous straws grasped concerns something called "the agonic line." This is the line of zero magnetic deviation, formed by linking spots where true north and magnetic north are the same direction. (Most places they aren't.) Causing, maybe, the slip nixed the plane and the ship, the agonic line curls down across the tail of the Bermuda Triangle. It coils right through the configuration of the Great Lakes.

David Hatcher Childress (*Lost Cities of North and Central America*) claims there are ancient submerged structures, even pyramids, in some of the Great Lakes, possibly reviving the "Atlantis-North" theory. Childress (a. k. a. "the gonzo archaeologist") is a fine tracker of folklore who does not always distinguish it dramatically from fact.

Whatever energy or chaos there is here has a great soul singer to keep it company. It was into the Great Lakes Triangle that the late Otis Redding flew to his end. Those who doubt the Great Lakes Triangle should see Gourley's book. He's done the research; let it speak for itself.

M. I. B.'S AND UFOS

American imaginations have been swept into the high-tech mythology of the UFOs as by no other form of folklore. There *might* be some legitimacy to the question, but we are so suspicious of reports that coincide with a modern media craze that it takes a lot of persuading to get us interested. Nevertheless, we can hardly ignore the matter. A couple of patterns about the Western Door emerge.

The "Niagara Corridor" is called one of the most UFO-ridden zones in the United States. Electrical disturbances have been associated with UFOs ever since the 1950's, and the East coast power blackout of Nov. 9, 1965 started with the sightings of a red oval object over power lines and funny lights about Niagara Falls. Whatever it was, something sucked up 200,000 kilowatts, crashed the entire system, and put 26 million people into the dark.

Less prominent in ancient tradition but hot in the modern is a stretch of mountain range (including the Allegany Reservoir) known as "Chestnut Ridge." (On the map this looks like a straight shot south down from the Niagara River.) This narrow course runs largely in Pennsylvania, though its roots are in the Southern Tier of the Western Door. It holds a grab-bag of modern myths: Bigfoot, UFOs, vortexes, crazy critters, and anomalies of all sorts.

Some individual sightings about the Western Door have been impressive. Charles Fort (1874-1932, "the father of American phenome-nalism") mentions several mysterious flying objects spotted well before the high-tech era. In 1828 Jonathan Bugbee - seriously lost in the then-formidable Cassadaga swamp - was guided to safety by what seems to have been a brilliant UFO. Among the papers of a prominent Buffalo family (in the possession of the Erie County Historical Society) is a UFO report from the 1940's accompanied by a rough sketch. Otherwise, most of the business falls into the two major zones.

The closest thing to a Western New York "Third Kind" encounter we've heard of took place near Cherry Creek in Chautauqua County. Sources differ as to the exact date, though most put it in October 1965. A slow-moving, vividly colored UFO neared the ground, perhaps even touching down near a farm as a teenaged boy watched. A tractor powering milking machines suddenly stopped. A bull tethered to a metal pole struggled and bent it 45 degrees. Something gooey, purple, and gross was left on the ground. The matter was investigated by the State Police and the US Air Force.

There may or may not be a real "X-Files" division of our FBI, but for awhile now we've been catching wind of an investigation that went on in connection to the Cherry Creek UFO. What we've not heard of is a coverup. The investigation of the State Troopers was overseen by the man - a retired State Trooper - to whom we spoke. This gentleman simply told us that a confusing matter had once come before him. He gave us the facts as he knew them. They are as we have reported.

The "MIB's" ("Men in Black") are stiff, dark-suited guys in sunglasses who drive big dark cars. Sometimes they show up in out-of-the-way locations in black helicopters. They typically interrogate and sometimes even threaten people who report UFOs. It's not clear whether they're part of the cure or the disease. Formerly elements of cult folklore, they'll soon be legendary in a mass sense. A blockbuster movie turning the "Men in Black" into good guys came out just before this book saw print.

Black helicopters have been reported in the Southern Tier after particularly distinct UFO sightings. According to some local UFOlogists, harassment from the MIB's caused at least one UFO research group (there were prominent ones in Rochester, Buffalo, and Jamestown) to go under. Allegedly the ringleaders no longer return phone calls from their former associates.

We would like to emphasize again the many classic mythic elements that seem to enter into the UFO phenomenon. UFO "abductions" (as revealed under hypnosis) are basically high-tech revisitings of the old fairy captivity motif in European folklore. Big light discs in the sky are mandala-symbols (images of wholeness in Jungian psychology) found in ancient art worldwide. This would be a suspicious series of events were the phenomenon wholly technological.

MYSTERY MONSTERS

Freaky furries are common in modern legend. Probably the best-known of the American ones is "Bigfoot," an apelike giant commonly associated with the southwest, but spotted in most wooded states of the Union. To go with all the hallucinogenic whoppers, there are centuries of verbal testimony and some good evidence: a film, recorded sounds, and many footprints. (These have been subjected to close analysis, and it is impossible to prove fraud.)

Equally curious are the "Big Cat" sightings in Britain. These, too, sound almost too wild to consider, except for the evidence. The very elusiveness of the critters - like Bigfoot - is mind-boggling, and inconsistent with signs of their physical existence that include frayed farm animals and some good photographs. We'll mention a few Western Door contributions to the "crazy critter" file.

Stories about a giant bear come to us from the Allegany region, but they sound more like campfire tales than serious sightings (or hallucinations). After some sort of incident in August 1946 in Busti, there was a panther scare that continued and grew for weeks complete with sightings and tracks. From the Franklinville area come some modern reports (reminiscent of those in the UK) of a strange big cat: tracks, searches, victims, some good sightings, and its unearthly cry. The last two panthers in Buffalo were allegedly shot by "Kenjockety" (the last of the Kaquahs, or Neutral Nation), back in the early 1800's. There should have been no natural ones left in the entire Western Door by the twentieth century.

We've heard plenty of "Bigfoot" lore from the Southern Tier, particularly about the Allegany Reservoir and parts of Pennsylvania near it. Actually (according to Loren Coleman, *Curious Encounters*) the Allegany region seems more conspicuous for a "creature from the Black Lagoon" type of beastie, reported "in a watery line down the Susquehanna through the Southern Tier of Western New York." At least one modern woodsman (a NYS Conservation Naturalist, according to Coleman) whose name we will mercifully withhold reported such a web-footer in 1977, "a scaled manlike creature that appears at dusk from the red, algae-ridden waters to forage among the fern and moss-covered uplands." It may be worth mentioning that the Kiantone community of Harmonia became convinced there were or had once been web-footers about the same general region. Such stories may be traceable to Cornplanter.

More crazy critter reports come from Livingston County. On October 12, 1870, the *Livingston Republican* ran an article about a strange beast seen by several people. It was large, bipedal, and, from the description, a bit like a wacked kangaroo. The late-nineteenth-century residents of Livingston County would have recognized such a beast, though, and this one's temper was not that of an herbivore. It attacked a number of dogs, rearing on its back legs and striking out with its forepaws.

A few weeks later, another article claimed that the beast "literally tore the feet and ears" off a pooch belonging to a doctor in Moscow. On the last day of 1870 the *Nunda News* reported what had to be the same strange animal, spotted outside of Moscow (now the village of Leicester). The accounts make no mention of critical details: its skull size and shape, its tail or lack thereof. They describe its motion as virtual hopping, and its pawprint like that of a dog.

No sightings of the Livingston County Bigfoot seem to have followed, but within a few weeks the jokers were out. A local wag (of the pseudonym "Sugarberry") wrote a developing series of editorials pretending to be monster-tales, luring the reader in until finally revealing that the skulking baby-eater was a local politician. As far as we can tell the early reports were serious.

SECRET SERPENTS

The Iroquois have some prominent tales of big serpents. Their thunder-being was involved in a running duel with the great horned serpent, a cycle of tales culminating in the critter's death near Niagara Falls. The Seneca creation myth stars a mighty, man-eating snake near their hill of origin at the top of Canandaigua Lake. It's hard to know what else to make of these tales, but we would not look for literal truth behind any myth, particularly one so archetypal. (Some implications of the story are discussed in the final chapter of this book.)

The Western Door has had a number of USO (Unidentified Swimming Object) sightings. We know of several reports between 1817 and the 1980's of something big and slithery in Lake Erie near Dunkirk. Rosemary Ellen Guiley (*Atlas of the Mysterious in North America*) reports that the Lake Erie serpent has been seen intermittently since 1819. She even gives a description: dark brown with a light underside, thirty-five to fifty feet long, with fins, a pointed tail, and a doglike head. She also describes a Lake Ontario mermaid (or merman) sighted in 1813. It was the size of a seven year old, with a clearly visible humanlike upper body. Right.

The world's most famous mystery water monster - that of Loch Ness, nicknamed "Nessie" - inhabits a fairly small lake, but recent studies of the loch's dimensions (as well as its supply of fish and plant life) do not rule out the existence of a big predator. Some of the sightings in Western New York come from such small bodies of water that we have trouble even considering them. (Several reports have come from Findley Lake, one from the summer of 1883).

The Silver Lake serpent (first observed on a Friday the thirteenth in 1855) was almost certainly a fake, despite the old Seneca legend about it. We say "a fake" because, in 1857, a fire wrecked a house on the shores of small, cold Silver Lake and a crude replica of a dragon was found. We say "almost certainly" because, though the fake snake was found, human fakers often get into the act after a possibly real phenomenon. (The crop circles of England come to mind.)

Probably the most persuasive of the local serpent legends is the one from Seneca Lake, a body already known for another curiosity, a loud, infrequent, apparently natural sound effect called "the Seneca Lake Guns," for which there is still no confident theory. (According to Arthur Parker, the Iroquois refer to "underwater drums" to explain a similar effect in Cayuga Lake.) One hot Summer afternoon in 1900, a boatload of reliable witnesses encountered something physical and living. The story is all too human and a little bizarre.

The passengers aboard the side-wheel steamer *Otetiani* noticed a big object 400 yards or so ahead. It was about twenty-five feet long, and they assumed it was a capsized boat. Captain Herendeen scanned it with his telescope, then gave the order to slow down. When the *Otetiani* was about 100 yards away, they were surprised to note the thing move.

The boat set off in pursuit, and in a little while the object turned its head back and flashed a mouthful of gnarly pearlies. Several prominent citizens of Geneva (including the police commissioner and the manager of the phone company) reported all this as fact to the *Rochester Herald*. A geologist gave us the best description of the beast: a triangular four-foot head, a long mouthful of sperm-whale like teeth, a horny turtle-like skin, a creamy belly, and fishy lidless eyes. He suggested it might be a *clidastes*, a type of extinct aquatic lizard.

The captain of the *Otetiani* was confronted with something entirely unknown to him. Naturally (or should we say, "humanly"), he decided to kill it; the boat's second pass at the strange critter, which was probably sick or injured anyway, caught it with the starboard paddlewheel, knocking passengers off their feet and a big hole into the critter's side. Its spine broken, the poor relic breathed its last. In minutes, boats were lowered and ropes slung about it, but a slip of the tail through one noose cast its whole weight onto the others. The Seneca monster slid into the 600-foot depths of the lake.

A week after the event, the *Geneva Gazette* suggested that the whole thing was a hoax. The *Geneva Daily* made no mention of it at all, but referred obliquely to the heat of the preceding week, and the drink and hallucination to which it had driven many Genevans. To counter the japing papers, however, we have the testimony of the *Otetiani* passengers and crew. In addition, many Seneca Lake residents have claimed that large unknown shapes have been seen about their long, deep lake. We are left with little else to judge the tale.

THE BYRON EARTH WHEELS

[We've heard of "crop circles," but "earth wheels"? How else to describe them?]

On March 20, 1920 the *Batavia Daily News* carried an article on strange natural doings. The fall before a round hole thirty feet deep had appeared on the Dillingham farm west of Byron. Another descending pattern of earth, described as "a drop of many acres," happened south of Attica in the same season. Conjecture seemed to satisfy itself with the "underground water" theory, but that was not involved in the article's main feature.

Sometime in the middle of March, John Webber walked to the far eastern edge of his Byron farm to check on a big drain. He saw something odd. A chunk of his thickly growing wheat field had been picked up and moved nine feet to the east. This formation was about fourteen feet across, sixteen to twenty inches deep, and circular in shape. The earth moved had been lifted right down to hard pan. The big section was estimated to weigh ten tons. Small sections of it had broken off.

One reason it was so quickly spotted was the massive, inexplicable hole. Even so, it would have been noticeable because the section had been rotated. Its rows of wheat were no longer parallel with those of the field, which had been running northwest and southeast. A smaller chunk about two feet by six had also been moved and rotated about ninety degrees. Another, only a wheelbarrow full, had been moved eastward about eighty feet. It was a gentle genie that had moved the big part, and a curious explosion that had scattered the rest. The fact that the growth of wheat on the migrating earth wheel was the same height as that in the rest of the field led many to believe the shuffle had come after winter set in.

Huge discs of earth missing from the landscape have been reported in parts of Canada, but otherwise we've heard of nothing like the Byron earth wheel. The matter puts us in mind, though, of the famous crop circles, most commonly found in England and other North Atlantic countries. They've been reported about the Western Door, though to little stir. In 1990 one was observed on an Eden ridge near a likely spot - Crystal Hill, Dan Winter's mystical homesite. We hear that in the early 90's a crop circle was found near Medina, and pretty well trampled by the time a team got there to test it. Our sources tell us fakery could not be proved.

Modern hoaxers are well into the business, particularly with the more elaborate crop circles. It's fairly easy to tell the difference between the forged ones and the inexplicable: in the former, the stalks of grain are broken by sheer force; in the latter, they are smoothly curved as if they simply grew, or swirled, into their new directions. It's hard to see how the latter process could be faked.

     Crop circles may not be new. Old woodcuts seem to depict the same thing, often attributed to fairies. One witness in the British Isles who filmed an area that shortly after developed a crop circle believes a light in the center of the field was the sign of a UFO that made it. We have heard of subtle, mysterious lights in areas soon to develop crop circles, but it still confounds us that these totally terrestrial, relatively simple artifices are interpreted as coming from beyond the earth. Since these natural patterns speak to the deep unconscious, many interpret their proliferation in recent decades (now that the world is in such dire ecological peril) as some kind of message, perhaps of alarm. If so, they may represent the last gentle signals we will receive. We cannot help but wonder if the unexplained spherical pattern of Byron in 1920 may be some form of the same phenomenon, if we could only figure out for sure what that is.

ROCKY RAIN

[One of Charles Fort's specialties was crazy showers from the sky. There have been several about the Western Door, according to Janet and Colin Bord: fishfalls at Buffalo in 1900 and 1939, and at Niagara Falls in 1933; and cardboard-like substances at Elmira in 1956. Had Fort only been around for this one!]

In November of 1973 an inexplicable shower of rocks fell for several nights upon the Greece home of the Frank Marella family. The rocks were of variable sizes, though none were bigger than baseballs. They came from all directions, largely at 45-degree angles. They left gashes on the sides of the house and broke windows.

Of course the authorities checked into every imaginable possibility; human pranksters, even slingshot artists, was the first that came to anyone's mind, despite the unlikelihood of so many hurlers staying hidden. The police sealed off the neighborhood during a siege and hunted. Not only was the search fruitless, but the rocks came down as it transpired. As a final indignity, the stones even hit police cars. The police-men themselves simply stared, or dove for cover.

In five nights the miracle was over. Six years later, Mrs. Marella confessed to the *Rochester Democrat and Chronicle* that the matter had her at her wits' end. It would have done worse to most others.

We know of no explanation for strange falls of objects like those observed by earlier anomalists like Charles Fort and contemporaries like Arthur C. Clarke. These object-showers range from the common (stones) to even the comestible (nuts). Even living rains - fish or frogs - have been recorded throughout the last two centuries, and, unlike ghost sightings, plenty of evidence is left behind.

In *Unexplained Mysteries of the 20th Century*, Janet and Colin Bord note something similar to the Rochester incident not too far away. In October 1973 some fishermen in their boat on Skaneateles Lake were besieged by gentle falls of pebbles. They got ashore without incident and drove to a pub in Liverpool. The unlikely precipitants rained on them again when they came out. Study showed that the small rocks were of local origin.

Any conjecture we have about the trouble in Greece would be grasping at straws. We'd like to know more about the site; some faint clue may lie there. This "rocky rain" sounds like a psychic event, maybe a prodigious PK (psycho-kinetic) display. The fact that no one, apparently, was hurt in such a drastic interchange may heighten that possibility. The spooks don't seem to hurt anyone. They can scare the bejeeping bozabbers out of you.

SPOOK HILL

Geomagnetic anomalies are familiar to the practitioners of orthodox science. They also enter the speculations of many modern New Age mystics. In the American west there are said to be several locations where compasses go crazy, electronics misbehave, and gravity rebels. (The "Zone of Silence" in the Mexican state of Chihuahua is another storied prodigy, but sinister.) For a time it seemed that a section of dirt road near the Yates County town of Middlesex might be among them.

"Spook Hill": the name itself, though meaning merely a road where kids on bikes think they coast uphill, is a testament to the way the general public associates anything strange with anything paranormal. It's like another stereotype we commonly encounter, that of associating anything paranormal, like ghosts, with anything evil, like Satan. We often interview people who presume that the specter of a departed relative can and should be warded with crucifixes and garlic. This baffles us. (The author's departed relatives, should they return, would mean no one harm.) But on to Spook Hill.

In 1976 David Dutton (physicist and research scientist at the University of Rochester's Institute of Optics) took his instruments to this stretch of road called Spook Hill. He concluded, and we see no reason to disagree, that there is no miracle here. Bikes don't roll uphill; it only looks that way. An optical illusion is created by the environment of Spook Hill. The contrast between a long steep climb suddenly leveling may make a very gentle upward slope look as if it slopes down. The visual effect is encouraged by the telephone poles on Spook Hill, which actually lean about four degrees in concert.

Spook Hill is among the valleys near Canandaigua Lake, near Native American burial ground. There may be other paranormal rumors about this site we have not heard, and there are certainly other alleged earthy anomalies about the Western Door which at another time we may discuss. Spook Hill, it would seem, has been laid to rest.

PITTSFORD'S MYSTERIOUS TUNNELS

No one alive has entered them, though we do not doubt they are there. We know of no sure entrances, though one is rumored beneath a legendary troubled house. They were almost certainly not man-made, but who can say? Though several high school classes have made it their very public project in the last few decades, this longstanding mystery is no closer to being solved.

A number of things convince us that a large underground cavern is beneath the four corners area of Pittsford. Several village residents of the past century and earlier in this have discovered and even walked about it. Digging and renovation in the area has indeed opened up what seemed to be passages under the surface. A bulldozer almost fell through. Many old houses (perhaps even linked to each other by the tunnels) have bricked-up doorways below ground.

The village of Pittsford tops limestone strata, and the Genesee River is not far off. The action of water upon soft mineral could be a natural explanation for the tunnels and cavern underneath the four corners area. Though there was probably "underground railroad" activity in Pittsford in the middle of the nineteenth century, these tunnels may have no connection.

Ancient people attached spiritual significance to the ground above caves and other peculiarities. Many famous temples are sited above such features, and paranormal lore often draws to them. Were these caves known to the Native Americans? Were there shrines and legends about this area too? What's really down there?

There are many ghost stories about Pittsford, some from the cemetery near the center of the town. One Pittsford house reputedly haunted is at 52 South Main Street, above the fabled entrance to the tunnels. This was the Hargous House, built in 1814 by Augustus Elliot. It was intended as a home for him and his bride-to-be, but she left him and married another. Elliot sold the house, but locals explain the presence encountered there as the ghost of his lost love. This seems an odd candidate for a haunter, haunting the house she rejected in life. Maybe the effect of the tunnels confuses living and dead.

NIAGARA FALLS

Iroquois shamans sacrificed food and goods here. The first Whites who beheld it merely stood and gaped. Modern psychics say anyone who listens long enough can hear ancient spirits clearly and well. In Six Nations folklore, the giant snake - their image of the earth-force, by all accounts - figures prominently here, coming to his epic contretemps with Heno, their Thunder-Being.

Like all natural forces - fire, electricity, wind - this one can be negative, too. For some people it's still too much, and too many tempt death leaping over these falls. Goat Island in its shadow was sacred to the Iroquois, who believed the Devil's Hole Cavern above the rushing river not far off was a haunt of their "Evil One." Snakes were often seen about this cave mouth, sunning themselves in legions after the long Western Door winter. Explorer La Salle may have been cursed here in 1687 and came later to a bad end. Two detachments of British troops were massacred by the Iroquois in 1763. Freak accidents happen here still with a depressing regularity.

We've already mentioned the prominence of "the Niagara Corridor" in the UFO cycle. Southern astrologer Steve Nelson points out that waterfalls were sacred all over the world, natural energy transformers and images of the dissolving process in alchemy. They are purifying in emotional senses, one reason the Falls are so traditional for lovers and newlyweds: their transforming energies can dissolve rigid patterns, either old patterns in the lovers' relationship, or old patterns of living apart. The mighty Falls can be their new beginning.

Anyone who doubts the Falls' mystic significance should only think of the famed "Harmonic Convergence," almost singlehandedly launched by art historian Jose Arguelles, author of a popular series of books mixing Mayan mysticism into New Age tradition. On August 16, 1987, the planets fell into the shape of a double-triangle "Star of David." A philosophical Woodstock was declared, a worldwide Vulcan mind-melt involving thousands of people aimed at solving the earth's problems. Certain sites of natural mystery and world-famous religious significance were chosen for the first dawn of the New Age. Among the worldwide elect: Macchu Pichu, Peru; the Great Pyramid; Stonehenge; Mount Olympus in Greece; Mount Fuji in Japan; and the banks of the Ganges in India. The fact that Niagara Falls ("one of the major power points") was among this august company should be all we need to hear.

TEN CLASSIC SPOOKS

MARTHA MATHEWSON

The English-speaking world of the nineteenth century did not put immortality on the same plane of reality as mortality but on a far higher one.

Derek Jarrett

NINETEENTH-CENTURY HAUNTINGS

About a century ago Sir J. G. Frazer (*The Golden Bough*) conjectured that humanity's first religious stirrings were rooted in their fear and awe of the human dead. Though we have mentioned before the broad range of modern paranormal interests, we cannot overlook the one that comes first to the mind of the average reader: ghosts, preferably in old, drafty buildings.

One of the first things that impresses the visitor about many reputedly haunted old sites is "feel" - an aura of something different. It may seem "evil" to some (usually only after hearing the tales); to others, this atmosphere of architecture and environment is sanctified, even "churchy." We note the suspiciously high number of old sites in the Western Door that seem to tally with the conventional "earth mysteries" checklist: religious significance, geological and astronomical distinctiveness, and the usual familiars (patterns of trauma and long habitation). The sites aren't just haunted; they're curious.

To some it might appear we've done a job of digging to produce our study of "Ten Classic Spooks." To the contrary; most of what we discuss has been discussed many times before. Our sites and events are often the most famous paranormal ones of their regions, some famous worldwide. Of course we came across a number of out-of-the-way tales, some most intriguing, but the tradition around them is less developed. When the only thing you have to make a case is oral testimony, there had better be a lot of it, and about most of the sites in this chapter there are generations.

In the Victorian era supernaturalism revived as a profession and was born as a study. In its century-plus of official existence, parapsychology has not made the strides for which its founders hoped, but one of the key arguments of its early days against the "material" theory of the universe remains the same: Someone trying to defy your statement that all crows are black doesn't need to prove that all crows are white, only that one of them is. We need only demonstrate one legitimate instance of psychic phenomena, anywhere or anytime in the world, to show the end of an old theory and the need of a new study. Little wonder that materialism's defenders are so vigilant. Parapsychology begins with the search for "white crows." There may be one or two in this gallery of the Western Door's classic hauntings.

FORT NIAGARA

[Fort Niagara and the "French Castle" within it are probably the most famous "haunted" sites about the Western Door.]

The high ground over the Niagara's outlet into Lake Ontario - practically a stone's throw to the Canadian shore - is a natural for castle-building. French explorer La Salle noted the strength of the site, selecting the eastern bluff of the Niagara's mouth for Fort Conti in 1679. This fortress was abandoned in just a few years, but several others followed. The French constructed Fort Niagara, whose oldest building, the "French Castle," dates from 1726. It was within easy view of beacons from a number of other colonial forts.

Fort Niagara is on top of up to a hundred structures. One source states that the earliest of twelve known forts was built around 160 A.D. by some Native American culture. Ray Wigle, Manager of Operations of Fort Niagara, informs us that the Fort's current archaeologists are aware of nothing resembling a Pre-Columbian fortress. Skeletons found here showed that their possessors had been cremated, possibly by the local priesthood or conquerors of the site.

Fort Niagara's odd, asymmetrical shape seems to serve no purpose but adapting to the physical traits of the site. The rectangular Castle (the main residence of the Fort) is the site of most of the stories. Six prominent ghosts figure in a century and a half of lore:

The headless ghost of the well

The hobgoblin of the "black hole" (the cell of solitary confinement)

The hobgoblin in the cemetery (first reported in 1815)

William Morgan's ghost in the powder magazine (He probably was held here. See "Track of the Illuminoids.")

The spectral French Count (first mentioned in 1863)

The lighthouse keeper (no twentieth century sightings)

Onondaga chief "Aaron" whose blood still stains the wall of his cell (It's rustoleum; and Aaron died of illness, not suicide, in the chill cell.)

"The headless ghost" is doubtless the Fort's best-known supernatural actor. The most basic tale is set during the French occupation of the Fort (1726-1759), and it involves a midnight duel between two officers over a Native American maid. The girl's favorite was winning, but he slipped and was run through. His head and body were separated, the former pitched into Lake Ontario, the latter down the Castle's twenty-five-foot-deep well. Ever since, the lidless ghost appears on nights of the full moon, searching for its missing part.

Some say this legend was already old when it first appeared in Samuel De Veaux's 1839 guidebook, but there's no mention of any Fort ghost before 1835 (in the diary of Mrs. Jewett, wife of the commander). De Veaux did stay at the fort before the War of 1812, maybe as early as

1802, when he might have picked up the story. There are, however, only American sources for this ghost tale, and no evidence of any sort for such a duel. A swordfight in the crowded Castle (officers' quarters by the 1750's) would hardly have gone unheard, and a bleeding body in the well would have shown itself in the breakfast tea. Neither would have escaped the records.

None of this hurt the story, rewritten and embellished many times in the century and a half since De Veaux's guidebook. Reporters looked into the matter in 1989 and found no sightings of "The Ghost of the Haunted Well." None. It seems that it's a figment of folklore, and, similarly, there are nothing but second-hand tales to support any of the other ghosts. That's an odd profile for a "haunted" site.

On the other hand, the Castle has supernatural earmarks. Many people on the Fort's staff get creepy feelings, and some parks police refuse to go in it alone at night. People who slept there received impressions of "presences" and heard sounds suggesting the Fort's early days. A newspaperman spent the night in the Castle in 1959 and related a smorgasbord of paranormal sound effects: falling kitchenware, "rattling chairs," opening and closing doors, praying soldiers, snoring sleepers, and marching footsteps.

In April 1980 nine investigators passed a night in the Castle with cameras, tape recorders, and psychics. They recorded nothing for posterity, though the two psychics experienced their strongest reactions to the one chamber in the building with its original flooring.

Buffalo's Channel 2 tried again in 1984. Tape recorders picked up some distinct, inexplicable noises: three loud footsteps and an old-time thumb-latch opening a door. Channel 2 ran the bit for two days.

A former Fort historian recalls a TV crew's late-1980's visit to a room in the Castle, during which no one present noticed anything out of the ordinary. On the videotape, however, a filmy, ectoplasmic, inexplicable shape flitted about behind the scene's human participants.

None of this supports the tale of the headless ghost or any of the other paranormal presences. The media record seems to suggest that there may be some supernatural effects at Fort Niagara, but certainly none in keeping with the more developed stories. If the Fort's supernatural environment was a rain forest, we, the observation team, have experienced background noise; we have trapped no jaguars.

CASPER MEETS RONALD MCDONALD

Lewiston's 1824 Frontier House is one of the Western Door's oldest buildings, once the western stop of the Barton Stage Line hosting some famous people: James Fenimore Cooper, President McKinley, DeWitt Clinton, Henry Clay, Washington Irving, and maybe the mysterious William Morgan, famed Batavia anti-Mason whose 1826 disappearance we discuss elsewhere. If Morgan was ever here, he was experiencing all the luxury the region could show, the day's finest accommodation west of Albany.

Rumor holds that it's Morgan's ghost stalking his murderers through this former Masonic meeting hall. (Funny. He was trying to get away from them when last we heard of him.) When the Frontier House was remodeled in 1963, many were disappointed that the body of Morgan (the Jimmy Hoffa of the mid-nineteenth-century) was not found.

The best modern lore about the site predates its McDonald's incarnation. The Frontier House manager had plenty to say to the Niagara Gazette in 1978. Apparitions and sound effects (like opening and closing doors in the empty building) make the usual paranormal pattern. A cleaning woman often talked with a man (in old-timey clothing) she encountered in the nooks, crannies, and closets of the place. A maintenance man quit over related creepiness. The manager himself was once shocked out of his shower by someone outside the steamy panels; he knew he was alone in the building. Animals have long been thought sensitive to super-natural presences, and the husky of the Frontier House chef got into the act, showing alarm and even hostility toward what was, to humans, vacant space.

The site's 1977 refashioning into the McDonald's franchise, one might think, would lessen its psychic vigor. (The glass-and-plastic imagery of fast-food culture would seem as dampening to native spirituality as an exorcism.) Yet in the late-70's both employees and workmen at the building sensed it was still psychically active: missing tools, misplaced items, and mysteriously opening windows.

Some who work at the Lewiston McDonald's still consider it haunted, due to unexplained phenomena of the familiar sort. We hear that Morgan and Fort Niagara's headless ghost meet routinely after hours at this apparent nexus for the malcontents of the local hereafter. We put no faith in the rumor that they were spotted force-feeding Happy Fries to some red-haired freak of a clown.

THE HYDESVILLE KNOCKINGS

[Supernaturalism has never really left humanity, and the first stirrings of another revival came to an Arcadia Township cottage in 1848. The cycle that started a few miles south-east of Rochester would help shape this world's attitudes to the next.]

For several nights loud, sporadic rappings had kept them awake, but John and Margaret Fox had no one but themselves to blame. Rumor held that their cottage was haunted, and the previous tenant had left with similar complaints. On the last night in March 1848, the pounding was so loud that father John made a thorough search of the soon-to-be-famous home. Daughters Margaret and Kate (fifteen and twelve) observed as he tested first this and then that fixture of the leaky house to see if it and the early spring wind might have co-conspired into percussion. Young Kate noticed that, as her father rattled a window, the sourceless sounds seemed to reply.

That night the Fox family went to bed early in the same room; the noises came again. "Here, Mr. Splitfoot, do as I do!" chirped Kate, clapping her hands. Despite being called an old name for the devil, the source of the sounds gave forth. "No, do as I do," cried Margaret, and the sounds played to her as well. "Is it a human being who makes these raps?" Mrs. Fox asked. No reply. She followed up: "If it is an injured spirit, make two raps." Those that answered shook the house.

Through a simple code devised on the spot the knocker announced that he had been a traveling salesman murdered in that very cabin. He had no objection to witnesses, and soon tense neighbors packed the house. He rapped his saga out.

The spook knew things no one there could have, even if he or she had been able to tap them out in a houseful of canny farmfolk. He revealed his name, and even accused the cottage's former occupant of his murder. (This was John Bell, who indignantly defended himself with a letter of good character signed by his new neighbors.) The spirit seemed to have covered all his bases, however, having already foretold that his murderer would never be called to earthly account.

The press had a party with the tale. The girls left the cottage; the rappings followed to the home of older sister Leah, becoming widely known as "The Rochester Knockings." The old house at 167 Plymouth Avenue (on Corn Hill) became a virtual opera house of the afterlife, winning many converts for the sisters. [Corn Hill keeps its psychic rep, but the Foxes' lovely home (and the lovelier Spiritualist church on the same street) came down under "urban renewal."]

Their effects seemed marketable as well as portable. Leah Fox took over from there. The girls went on tour, charging fees to hear the rapping spook and setting off a wave of imitators. P. T. Barnum took them to New York City, where they went over big. As if the impulse had been lurking all the while, people across the Western world set to experimentation. A great many discovered their own psychic powers (or

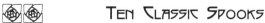

the like thereof). Mediums sprouted. (In Auburn, NY, there were no less than fifty in practice a year after the first New York displays.) Spirit speaking soon became a full-time job.

A new religion started declaring itself almost as soon as the Fox sisters went public. "Spiritualism" the nebulous young faith was called, with the Fox sisters as its virtual vestals. It was roughly based on the ideas of Swedish mystic Swedenborg and "channeled" books by living writers like Andrew Jackson Davis. Movements and communities formed under gurus like John Murray Spear and Thomas Lake Harris of the Western Door, and John Humphrey Noyes in nearby Syracuse. To many, simply observing a seance was equal to attending a service of the new religion. Soon a public for whom the faith of the New Testament was too detached responded eagerly to one they need not wait until the last trumpet to behold. A few years after its birth Spiritualism boasted two million disciples.

In 1854 Congress tabled a petition urging that Spiritualism be the subject of a national inquiry. Cornelius Vanderbilt summoned mediums after personal tragedy, as did J. J. Astor. Mary Todd Lincoln had a spiritual advisor, and her husband "the Great Emancipator" may have been more than just a bystander. Harriet Beecher Stowe was known to attend a seance now and again, and one famous New York session with the Fox sisters included Horace Greeley, William Cullen Bryant, George Ripley, and James Fenimore Cooper.

Many influential people were associated with Spiritualism, including many American Transcendentalists. Nathaniel Hawthorne was not very impressed by spirit-rapping in 1858, though it seemed to him genuine. Ralph Waldo Emerson respected Spiritualism, but thought its displays "the rathole of revelation." If the rappings at the average seance indicated the standard of after-living, the ever-sanguine Henry David Thoreau offered to trade his own afterlife someday for a glass of cold beer pronto. English poet Robert Browning satirized the great psychic D. D. Home as "Mr. Sludge," but snarled after one of his levitations, "I can't think how the thing was done."

Spiritualism identified itself with many social and political move-ments - like womens' causes and abolition - and in general seemed an enlightening force upon society. But like many of the traveling Victorian-era psychics the Fox sisters make a depressing tale. Overwhelmed either by the success of their profession or by its stress, both Kate and Maggie were "dipsomaniacs" (as a writer of their day put it) by their early twenties. They died from the effects of the hooch in their fifties. What concerns us is the possible legitimacy they may ever have had as the mediums or producers of psychic effects.

There are several variables in the debate. The Fox sisters were allegedly caught a couple of times faking sounds. [Three University of Buffalo professors declared that the women could not produce psychic effects when their feet were tightly held, and deduced that somehow (perhaps by dislocating their big toes) they'd faked them all along.] Also, searches beneath their cottage not long after their first effects had turned up little hard evidence of a buried peddler. [The diggers stopped when they encountered flowing water, which makes us suspect a geomantic ("earth magic") significance to the site.] Kate and Margaret even confessed to chicanery late in their lives. To most skeptics, this is enough and plenty to end interest in the case. We're not so sure.

It's not pretty when a psychic is caught in deception, and it will always imply to eager skeptics that anything he or she ever did must have been faked as well. Yet the original manifestations in the Fox cottage of 1848 seemed to include poltergeist effects no children could have staged. It takes less work to think of them as supernatural.

Controversy surrounds the matter of the "murdered peddler" whose spirit-knockings were supposedly behind it all. In 1904 after the last of the Fox sisters was dead, some decomposed human remains were found beneath their former cottage behind a false wall. This had fooled the first diggers, and it appeared that someone had gone the extra mile to hide them long before. Even traces of a peddler's box were found near the bones, supporting the story of the knockings.

It's hard to be sure the confessions make a simple issue, either. At the time they "came clean" Kate and Margaret Fox were broke and ill, and the papers were paying for nothing but an expose. It's possible that their confessions were part of a feud with older sister Leah, and that each was drunk at the interview. These confessions were abruptly recanted and probably do not count for much, though they burned bridges with former supporters. A collection among the entire faith near her death found only $86.80 for Margaret Fox.

We'd like to believe there was at least a grain of legitimacy to the birth of Spiritualism. It would be a shame to think of so many people wasting their faith. The story of the Fox sisters and the early days of the traveling psychics is not always inspiring, but somewhere in it there may be a few white crows. It's that keeps us on the search that gave rise to this book.

THE BROTHERS DAVENPORT

[A new wave of supernaturalism swept with the Fox sisters out of the Western Door. Soon it was found that "the spirits" were more than a rhythm section. Levitating tables, disembodied voices, and spontaneously playing musical instruments became features of seances on both sides of the Atlantic. Trickery was rampant, most of it exposed in its own day, but several prominent American psychics were never convincingly discredited: the Fox sisters (at least before they went pro); D. D. Home, a transplanted Scot with seemingly prodigious powers; channeler and healer Andrew Jackson Davis; the ectoplasmic Ohio orchestra of the Koons family's "Spirit Room"; Vermont's miraculous Eddy brothers; and two sons of a Buffalo policeman - the Brothers Davenport.]

William and Ira Davenport - 14 and 16 years old at their Buffalo debut - had discovered their psychic abilities in a typical way for the day: they'd heard about the Fox sisters, wondered about their own chances of evoking the same effects, sat around a table with their family one night, and heard the first mysterious rappings. They started in 1855 by giving private demonstrations in which the spooks communicated through the code of raps (already familiar to the spirit-thirsty public) that had been customary since its devising for the Fox sisters. Soon a single spirit emerged, naming himself first "King Number One" and, more commonly, "Johnny King," and commanding the brothers to rent an auditorium and charge for admission. "King" (sort of a latter-day Robin Goodfellow who spoke through many other Victorian-era mediums) prescribed the construction of a light, portable cabinet, about seven feet by six by two, within which he and his band of spirits could stage their marvels. The undertaking was an immediate success, and "The Brothers Davenport" were launched.

Their demonstrations at first were typical of touring psychics in the middle 1850's: rappings, voices that spoke through a sort of trumpet, and levitating musical instruments (tambourines, bells, violins) that played inside their closed box. Yet the act of the Davenports progressed rapidly, often discovering new powers of the "spirits" by responding to audience requests. Like most of the convincing psychics of their day (as well as ours) the brothers were willing to be examined closely, almost as if they were curious about their own power. Like most psychics of any era, they liked dim lighting.

On their first trip to New York, Professor Loomis of Georgetown University's Medical College was one of three members of the audience picked to sit on stage. He provided what is still the best description of the Brothers' performance, which reached more or less its final form only a few months after their coming-out.

The New York reporters found the knocks, voices, and mysteriously playing instruments so spectacular that they suspected trickery, and wondered if "the spirits" could still make music were the brothers tied to their chairs. Neither the boys nor "Johnny King" objected, and with ropes and handkerchiefs the reporters set to work. The lights dimmed, the cabinet-doors closed, and the spirit-racket sounded again. Next, Professor Loomis sat in the box during the recital, with a hand tied to a leg of each brother (probably to restrain his own musical impulses). Soon after the doors closed, the instruments rose and played, even brushing Loomis as they levitated past him. There weren't enough material hands in the box, even unfettered, to play all the instruments.

When the cabinet doors opened, its three occupants were still at one with the woodwork. Someone asked spirit-master King if he could free them; he rapped his assent, the cabinet closed, and the crowd could hear the rope fairly humming as it was drawn through the arms and legs of the chairs. In a minute it was lying on the floor, every knot undone. The astonished reporters signed a paper stating that they could detect no fraud, and Professor Loomis proposed "the agency of a new force."

Loomis' oddest observation about this early performance was the appearance of spectral hands in and about the box, evidently responsible for the phenomena. This was to be reported many times at the displays of other psychics - including the twentieth-century Polish medium Franek Kluski.

The Davenports toured England with Southern Baptist preacher Jesse Babcock Ferguson. Sir Richard Burton observed and described their performances. Many attendees could not resist peek-a-boo, and all reported the same things: spirit-hands in and about the Davenports' box, of varying human size and shape: thin, female, childish, burly, pale, black, and all shades in between. One too-curious observer was slapped on the shoulder by a spirit-hand that seemed clearly disembodied. It was as if the brothers and their audience had become a petting-zoo for the multi-cultural residents of the hereafter. Often when matches were struck by would-be exposers, musical instruments fell straight to earth, sometimes injuring spectators.

The brothers' routine began to feature escapes. Celebrated and famous, for the next twenty years they toured the world, where many (including Emperors Alexander III and Napoleon III) were astounded. William proved a bit of a Romeo, even having a long affair with the glamorous actress Adah Isaacs Menken. The Davenports' performances were described in detail by newspapers on several continents. Spectators constantly tried to expose them; none ever did.

Some fellow psychics, however, were suspicious of the Brothers Davenport, who virtually never failed to perform. Even the wondrous D. D. Home never knew if a display of his own would be successful. One of the few times the brothers misfired was when three Harvard Professors (along with Louis Agassiz, the famous geologist) observed them in a mocking atmosphere, clearly more set on debunking Spiritualism than studying it. The Brothers were pinioned according to plan, but the spirit-orchestra failed to perform, and only one of the brothers, and only his upper body, was freed. This much would have been near-impossible for anyone else, but since the Brothers had failed to complete their performance, the professors crowed victory. Agassiz alone was not so sure this settled the entire question, either of psychic phenomena or of the Brothers Davenport.

Read several assessments of the brothers and you will find many points of disagreement. No better example is needed than the reaction to their other notable failure, a refusal to perform in Liverpool. Some writers presume that a special "Tom Fool's knot" prevented the brothers from freeing themselves to produce the other manifestations of their act. Others write simply that, in the initial process, a drunken spectator had pulled the ropes so excruciatingly tight that the brothers requested to be freed instantly, without waiting for the ceremony of the spirits. None disagree about the result, however: a brawl.

Some critical differences separated the Davenports' performances from other "escape" acts of their day and ours. Members of the audience led the process of fettering the brothers, which sometimes took forty-five minutes and involved all sorts of gimmicks. (The brothers were lucky an eyelid was left free to blink.) Spectators were allowed on stage, sometimes right in the magic box. The speed of everything the brothers did is also puzzling: it seldom took more than two minutes for them to escape the most intricate bonds. And the Davenport Brothers could go back in their box and somehow get tied up again, as thoroughly as before, and as quickly as they had escaped. Not even Houdini did that.

At least the earthly partnership between the brothers ended in 1877 when William Davenport died in Australia. Though the brothers had never directly stated whether they were authentic mediums or simply "magical" performers like Houdini or the Maskelyne brothers, the authorities in Sydney were convinced enough of their occult legitimacy to refuse William burial on hallowed ground. Ira (sleeping now in a Mayville, NY cemetery) lived till 1911 to the age of 70 and was befriended by Harry Houdini. The great escapist later claimed that, just before he died, Ira had confessed to a career of trickery. This is just a story, however; Houdini offered no proof for it.

British writer Sir Arthur Conan Doyle, an ardent believer who leaped to the defense of Spiritualism at every slight, countered Houdini's charge with one of his own: that Houdini was a gifted psychic whose escapes were done entirely with spirit-aid; Houdini's descriptions of the earthly methods behind his act, and his attacks on Spiritualism, were only to throw others off the trail. As Slater Brown has observed, these two still-famous men illustrate the regrettable extremes of attitude to psychic phenomena, and the whole skirmish between them is ironic: Houdini made other groundless assaults on spiritualism (such as claiming to be able to duplicate the marvels of D. D. Home); and, where spiritualist phenomena were concerned, the creator of Sherlock Holmes was famously blind to deception. Doyle's statement about Houdini's occult powers is probably no more backed by evidence than the latter's charge that the Brothers Davenport were total fakes. It may be safest to concede a few more things between Heaven and earth, including the Buffalo Brothers Davenport, than our science yet has philosophy for.

THE OCTAGON HOUSE

It defies the textbook wisdom on ghosts to think that one would follow a building to a new location, but that may be the case with Mumford's Octagon House, built about 1870 for Erastus Hyde. He and his wife were both devoted Spiritualists, holding many seances in their house in the small Allegany County town of Friendship. The couple died only two days apart in 1931.

The house passed through several owners. When it fell vacant, the stories started. Friendship folk heard strange sounds from within the darkened manse, and saw objects moving about of their own accord. Passersby saw the lone ghost of Mr. Hyde, and others noted spectral pow-wows, parliaments of spirits Hyde had once called down to speak when he was living. Now he could sit right beside them.

Today the Octagon House is in Mumford's Genesee Country Village, more or less a museum community illustrating pioneer life in this part of the state. When it was first moved here, the paranormal stories started again. Workmen reported their tools moving suspiciously. The director's dog would have nothing of the house, and a number of people - including a psychic called in to do a seance - had unsettling dreams and eerie feelings. Many visitors to the building made similar reports.

We're always impressed when paranormal lore falls into expected patterns. Though an old folk adage holds that spirits dwell in right-angle corners (which an eight-sided building might be thought to avoid), octagonal houses are commonly associated with paranormal lore. [As we see in paranormal realms, no rule is never broken (except maybe that one).] The eight-sided shape is often used in "sacred architecture," which has a tendency to gather supernatural rumor. We point out that Washington's Octagon House is reputedly one of our capitol's most haunted buildings.

A number of octagonal buildings are found about the Western Door. This form was advocated by Burned-over District mystic Orson Fowler (1809-1887), founder of several enlightened settlements. An octagon house was built in Lily Dale for the Spiritualist headquarters. Akron's Rich House is another, and we've heard of a modern community near Attica based around an octagonal structure. (No word yet if all of these are haunted.)

THE OLD MAIN STREET CEMETERY

The cabin was old when the Community of True Inspiration made their purchase in West Seneca (just outside Buffalo). The first legion of German settlers were obliged to use every bit of shelter standing on their chunk of the Buffalo Creek Indian Reservation, all twenty-nine buildings and one fateful cabin no Seneca grieved to leave.

By the 1840's the building had associations of evil, and deeds "shameful" and "outrageous" according to old documents. The Ebenezer family that moved in soon reported supernatural effects, including terrifying apparitions and sounds.

In June of 1845, Christian Metz (1794-1867), spiritual leader of the Community of True Inspiration, spent the night in said cabin, armed with what had to be ample faith in his own piety. In the morning he confirmed the hair-raising tales. He, too, experienced spectacular, hideous effects. He, too, saw a tortured spirit, a Native American woman in torment and chains. He proclaimed that the cabin should be burned and the ground consecrated. This was spiritedly done, and the site made part of the Ebenezers' own burial ground. But no one was ever buried on that precise spot - no one, perhaps, but its haunter.

Historian Frank J. Lankes did some poking around in the archives of the Amana Society (as the Ebenezers were known after their move to Iowa). He found what seemed to be a connection between their 1845 experience and a witchcraft incident of 1821. The "haunted" cabin had been that of a Seneca woman named Kauquatau, a healer who attended a sick Seneca man seeming to need only simple nursing. He died so strangely that the community suspected witchcraft. The woman fled to Canada, and a Seneca council prescribed the death penalty. A delegation of chiefs set out to convince her to return. They succeeded, and the minute they crossed the reservation boundary the executioner was expected to act. He quailed, due (according to rumor) to the "evil eye" the witch cast upon him. It was a chief called "Tom Jemmy" who drew his knife and slit the witch's throat. As if shocked at their own deed, they left her body where it lay, on the banks above the Cazenovia Creek.

The story of Tom Jemmy's trial (and Red Jacket's role in it) comes elsewhere in our study, but it seems that the woman had been suspected of witchcraft long before her death, and that she may have been buried beneath her cabin after. Obviously, no one mentioned this to the Ebenezers until they had begun to experience the frightening special effects. Knowing the Iroquois dread of witchcraft, historian Lankes conjectures that burial at her cabin would have been likely; no one else would want the unfortunate Kauquatau on their land, and at least that way the dubious spot would be well marked.

So far as we can tell, after Christian Metz' prescription was carried out the Ebenezer community was troubled no more by the offending spirit, though no one had anything to do with the site of the cabin burial ever after. Its exact location may never be known, but the Old

Main Street Cemetery was unusual for the square, vacant plot in the center once enclosed by a fence. No burials have ever been within it. Maybe there the evil house once stood.

This cemetery has a long record of twentieth-century ghost sightings, some of them written up in local papers. In September 1966 Buffalo reporter Dick Christian spent as much of the night as he could stand here, and fled after some suspicious sounds. A Spiritualist would probably conclude that the most likely source was the spirit of Kauquatau, failed healer and suspected witch.

Worse haunters are living. Though surrounded by pleasant houses now, the tiny open graveyard is vandals' victim. Most of its stone sentinels are fallen. Surely moments of self-recrimination have to be coming for thoughtless adolescents who, to offend the living, would desecrate the dead.

HILL OF THE HELLHOUNDS

South of East Aurora are the Holland Hills, beautiful green ridges streaking to the Alleganies. Hunter's Creek runs through them, a shale-bedded stream seldom deeper than a foot or two, seldom wider than a dozen yards. The most majestic views in the county are formed by this aged stream as it winds to its joining with the Buffalo Creek. Tiny cemeteries rest in the pines and maples over its banks.

Something up here sparks folklore. Most concerns a graveyard at the hilly top of Goodleberg Road and the creek nearby. A field slopes behind it, with woods and pond beyond them - unquestionably the scene of many natural hijinks. Generations from Holland, Iroquois, and East Aurora high schools partied out here among the stones. (Maybe that explains their wretched state!) As adults, these folk give us most of the lore, making it among the most devil-ridden tracts in Erie county.

Themes of generation (like in the visions and speeches of Macbeth) dominate: witches delivering stillborns, ghostly tots in white dresses, cemeteries filled with infants, and rumors of country abortionists. Actually, the burials are suspiciously young, and the worst of the grisly tales are true.

Sometime before the 1940's a country doctor on Hunter's Creek Road expanded his services to include abortions (proscribed functions in those days), a story that suggests why such emotion surrounds the matter today. We have no word on his bedside manner with adult patients, but his ministrations were invariably lethal to the unborn, whose bodies were buried about the ridge.

"What a piece of work is a man!" says Hamlet of humankind, infinite in potential because of our immortal soul. In the informal annals of witchlore, few ingredients were more potent than body parts from unbaptized infants. Unclaimed for the mighty God of the Christians, such essences were free power to aspiring mages. Courtesy of the country doctor, this hill was a generator.

Women too died during the process, and their bones filled the freelance graveyard the area had become. Some found their way into the stream, turning up in fishing lines; family dogs came home with others. Body parts were found about the doctor's home. He killed himself rather than live behind bars.

The country graveyard raises a curious front, a box of earth sided with long stone logs. The hundred-odd stones date from the earliest White settlement of the area, now so badly vandalized that only a handful stand. One young bloke we've heard of took home a piece of one as a trophy. He returned it soon after; it scared him, always warm, as if it had some heat source of its own.

Convincing spook stories come from this stretch of road. Some refer to the appearance of an adult male, something of whom (dress, grooming, even an antique tool in hand) suggests an earlier day. He walks the road a few seconds in bright daylight and vanishes. Only his clothes (and his disappearance, of course) seem unnatural.

More tales attach to the hill, bisected by a road so winding, steep, narrow, and gulching as to be nearly impassable in winter. There's gossip of old homesteads, clans that have lived in them since their settlement, sinister shrines among the trees, and collusion beyond the ordinary (namely witchcraft) passed on as family tradition.

Huge, speedy dark hounds, sometimes alone, sometimes in packs, figure in the lore of this hill and graveyard. On unlucky nights they can be encountered about the stones, the road before it, and the wood and pond behind. Their baying is unearthly, their movement unspeakably fast and smooth; their black coats glisten like vinyl, and their eyes are red or green, and luminous. A couple reports one flew into the path of their car; the impact was shocking, but when they inspected road and vehicle, there were no signs of such collision.

One of the most curious aspects of this story is that these great supernatural hounds are images from Old World folklore likely familiar only to scholars. They're unlikely bogies for west Atlantic lands: the Devil's Dandy Dogs, Gabriel's Ratchets, the Hounds of Hell, sent to earth to rustle sinners' souls (Old Scratch, it would seem, too busy reforming Welfare to do everything himself). Their eye-coloring is also suggestive, since green, or red and green together, was a sign of supernaturalism in the folk ballads of the British Isles, most of which are medieval at root. Green clothing, when not distinguished as grass-stained, suggested that its wearer was a member of the fairy race, or a human wizard. [Grass stains - as in "Lady Greensleeves" - meant illicit lovemaking in the woods, and implied (in the old blues motif) that the lord of the manor was getting a little help he really didn't need.]

At first we considered keeping the name of the little cemetery secret in the hopes of preventing further vandalism; but what worse could be done to it? And it may look out for itself. Among the younger set is the adage that anyone who maltreats the stones up there usually pays for it down the road. A strange sense of guilt seems to stripe the vandal as he or she (usually he) overturns a stone; it falls like the toll of a bell, and he wonders if something else is to come. Streaks of bad luck and even injuries follow, that the culprit afterward connects to that initial feeling. Visit, but leave it be.

FOREVER ON A FALL AFTERNOON

Some allegedly haunted sites can become quite famous with, apparently, no good evidence of paranormal activity. The rumors start, and after a few generations everyone turns around to notice the tradition in full flight. Even the natural facts involved in the ghost tales may be unverifiable or even false. Yet with the Pink House, there is no such problem. Something happened here.

This graceful Victorian house at the corner of West State Street and Brooklyn Avenue in the Allegany County town of Wellsville was painted pink at its 1869 christening, and pink it's been ever since. Its flamingo coloring and story-book design bring tourists to a gawking stop. It looks "like a wedding cake," according to writer Ben Fanton. Disappointed love is at the heart of the most common folkloric account of the Pink House haunting, an old story that goes as follows:

The wealthy family owning the Pink House had two grown daughters. The older was engaged; as she waited for the groom at the altar, he eloped with her younger sister. She drowned herself in the fountain on the Pink House grounds. Not many years later the couple came back to live with their two-year-old daughter. The ghost of the older sister began to appear by moonlight near the fountain that was its last living rest. Then it came to the couple's bed, waking them by dragging its long wet hair over their faces. Soon the child started to see it, even developing a fey attraction to her vanishing aunt. The girl withdrew, becoming strangely distant and detached from her parents. She seemed to prefer the company of her silent, usually invisible friend, who apparently persuaded her of a simple way never to part. One night the child wandered off. They found her in the fountain.

The grieving couple left. By the time they had inherited the house and returned to it, another young daughter came with them. The ghost again began to appear, but they would not lose this child! Thereafter they kept a light on all the nights the girl slept in that house. The ghostly aunt only came once - when the gas faltered.

The owner of the Pink House at the time of several mid-1980's articles was a granddaughter of its builder Edwin Bradford Hall. Florence Woelfel did not believe in paranormal rumor, but had no objection to checking into actual fact. There had indeed been trauma at her house, almost in the sense of a family curse. It had nothing to do with a love triangle, except that it wound three lifetimes' measure of torment into minutes.

Just before one on the afternoon of September 26, 1907, Hall's daughter, Mrs. J. Milton Carpenter, walked down the curved walkway in front of the Pink House to see her two-year-old daughter Beatrice, pale and still in the fountain. She had wandered away from her nurse and crib and found a deadly shimmering playspace. Her grandfather Mr. Hall was paralyzed in a wheelchair on the porch. The old gentleman rocked on his rests, watching whole the ordeal of his tiny girl, fixed in place like a stone. No one heard his shouts for help. One can only imagine his emotions. Mrs. Woelfel confirmed the tale; Beatrice was her younger sister. The cursed fountain was filled and removed.

In the mid-1980's its caretakers acknowledged that the Pink House had its share of creaks and groans, and it felt a good deal more comfortable when Mrs. Woelfel was around; but haunted? Not a bit of it. Yet they had to concede they had recently noticed an odd effect: a light appeared to have turned itself on in a room neither of them had entered.

There may still be local rumors attesting that the Pink House is a weighty paranormal site, and that apparitions and electrical effects continue. Rumors they may only be, though, based on rumors. When people who live in a house believe it is not out of the ordinary, our tendency is to agree.

Nevertheless, a world of psychic torment had to be condensed into a few moments of a September day. A mother approached a fountain to make for herself the worst discovery any mother can, and a man near the end of his long life and a girl who should have been at her beginning fooled fate together, linked whirling in their individual griefs for what must have seemed forever one fall afternoon. It would be all too natural were some supernatural expression to linger beyond, if any such thing is possible. The fountain, at least, is gone.

THE WHITE LADY OF IRONDEQUOIT

[We hardly knew where to begin with Rochester. The graceful city at the mouth of the Genesee has preserved its spectral legacy exceedingly well; this whole chapter could have been filled with it. In the last century the pale unliving must have virtually orbited Corn Hill and Paddy Hill. Cemeteries Mt. Hope and Holy Sepulcher sounded each a veritable "Beetlejuice." We introduce Monroe County's most dangerous ghost. Give her berth.]

She may be Rochester's best-known specter, yet we know little about her. If there is a real story behind the White Lady of Irondequoit (the Western Door's own "Lady of the Lake") we do not have it, but the reports of her from Durand-Eastman Park, the marshy territory at the north of the city, are old, and very vivid.

She rises in the fog, a Victorian Diana above the sheeny surface of the tender pool, light hair and ragged tatters waving, perhaps in a wedding-dress. To some she is beautiful and womanly, to others haggard and threatening. Two German shepherds are at her every stride, assisting her in lethal search. She is a killer, companied with killers, searching killers.

A host of Old World archetypes flow with her, though she has arisen in a land foreign to them and in imaginations where they have no conscious footing: like Jung's lorelei, like Keats' "La Belle Dame...," like Graves' Lyceia, she comes, a victimizer of men. Flanked by wolfy hounds like the huntress-goddess of the Greeks, colored in the hues of her moon, her mortal tale is far other.

They say she was a mother whose daughter was raped, drowned, and lost. She gave herself raging to the waters of Durand Lake, perhaps the better to unleash her vengeful spirit, guaranteed that way eternal thoroughfare in that limbo known to the Spiritualists (from which the delirious of the afterworld sometimes come back). The spectral mother returns in the summers to search for her child again... and revenge. She drifts with her lupine charges about this well-known lovers' lane, and though the young girls have nothing to fear from her, woe be, they say, to men she finds.

We know of no one who has seen her and no one she has surely killed, so perhaps her manifestations are no more. Maybe she merely tired of the fruitless wandering, or maybe she is sated on her prey. If so, we pity him or them; but were they the murderers of her child, of any child, she's an avenger we understand. It would not surprise us did some such righteous predator stalk all vicious human ones through whatever halls or shadows represent eternity for the justly damned.

GREEN ACRES

[Maybe others can feel confident about it, but we're leery of assigning name and identity to a "haunter" at active sites. To us the paranormal is such a mystery, such a flurry of inconsistent details, that the truth cannot be so tidy. Readers can decide for themselves if the haunter of Newfane's mansion has a name.]

If the friends and wellwishers of the Van Horn Mansion have anything to say about it, this building is one of the most paranormally active about the Western Door. They're a bit shy of appearing in print, which we understand, living in a society that ridicules "superstition." But (perhaps eager to solve the mystery for themselves) they've made a study of the site, and recorded a stack of psychic incidents perceptible to three of the five senses.

"Green Acres" was its name when James Van Horn and his family lived in their mansion on the Transit Road in Newfane. This must have been a good place for his sawmill, and he a good manager, for it made his wealth. It's well he waited until 1820 to construct his fine home; during the scuffle we call the War of 1812 the British burned his mill, and plenty else hereabouts.

The red brick mansion has had several uses in a hundred seventy-seven years, including a mid-twentieth century stint as a restaurant. By 1959 it had turned to apartments, but from 1967 to 1970 lay vacant, host of vandals and home to crows. In 1972 it was a home again, and five years after bought by Noury Chemical. In another decade it was donated to the Newfane Historical Society, which cares for it lovingly today.

The environs of the Van Horn mansion seem disarming, not sublime and Gothic. Though a short way north is Olcott and the brooding Ontario, the house is isolated in its modern setting, in a stark parking lot by a busy road. Few trees or other buildings are near either to lend intrigue or help pen its own within its odd boxy shape. About a hundred feet off is "Cemetery Orchard" and the marker of Malinda, wife of James Van Horn, Jr. The stone may mark either the spot of her rest or the blow (from a falling branch) that sent her to it, at twenty-one, in 1837. It's she many suspect is behind the haunting.

The apparitions include a man, a woman (both looking out of place in our century), and a mysterious child. Living children have had strong reactions to these presences. Adults have compiled the list. A sample:

A roofer almost fell to the ground upon noticing a woman looking at him out of the window of the empty house.

A motorist skidded to avoid a girl who ran from the mansion, then vanished. The same apparition has startled others.

Carpenters in 1978 fled when a person materialized out of a cloud in a bedroom. They wouldn't go back even to get their tools.

A man from Noury Chemical saw moving lights inside the dark mansion. He called help, posted guards, and searched. Nothing.

The children of a family who lived in it in the 1950's could not sleep in a certain room, claiming to be troubled by "the others."

One warm night in September 1970 a small band of psychic intrepids held their first experiment at the mansion. They reported many odd sounds (including human weeping), and a definite, drastic "cold spot" (one of the mansion's most persistent effects) that seemed to follow them outside, violently shaking the bushes.

That long first evening really heated up when the plucky band regrouped on a porch. Scratching sounds came from the other side of the door - the inside. Of course they threw it open several times and saw no one. The sounds always resumed. Someone thought of asking questions, and an impromptu seance began. How eerie that must have been, the rapping of someone or something behind a door inside a dark, deserted mansion! They claimed to be "Malinda," unhappy, frightened, but far from alone.

In later seances, sounds seemed to come from the center of a table between the sitters' hands, and a chair rocked of its own accord. Once the rapping claimed to be a little old lady named "Abigail," quite happy at Green Acres. The kind-hearted amateurs were left wondering who it is that cries. Is it "Malinda"?

Her name is suggestive - Malinda - and slightly outre, a funny way to spell "Melinda." The root mal- is an old one for evil in the Romance tongues; and we're reminded of Malinche, Cortez' Aztec-cursing concubine. She, - no love for her own culture that had sold her from princess to slave - more than anyone but the old killer himself, is to blame for Mesoamerica's disaster. Without her he'd have blundered into one or another pitfall, and its ravage wait a generation more.

Sweet Malinda, for whom do you grieve? Is it yourself, for the tender tragedy of your too-young setting-off? Let it be for the ungrieved dead, those who pass with no one mourning. At least someone loved you, enough to see to your treasured rest, enough to set your stone and send you with the best they could conceive:

Sleep, Malinda, sleep; sleep soundly here where flowers bloom and zephyrs sigh.
We may come to shed the tears that stream unbid from sorrowing eye.

THE SPIRIT WAY

LAURA WILDER

If you are ever offered your choice between being an occultist and a black-smith, choose the lighter job and enter the forge rather than the lodge.

Dion Fortune

THE TRUMPET OF A PROPHECY

Though it might seem to be the statement of this book, we've never said that Western New York was an overwhelmingly paranormal area. It may be, but we can't think of a way of comparing it with other regions; few studies like this one are ever done, and this type of lore thrives just about everywhere people live. Even the history books, however, notice the fever of religious energy about the Western Door. Surely, an unseemly number of prominent, largely countercultural religious movements, leaders, and communities have flowered in this small area. This we think is the Western Door's distinctive legacy. We note in this chapter group spiritual activity, the birth of faith, and the collection of the faithful. Most of it involved mysticism, and what we might call magic.

A large chunk of upstate territory including most of the Western Door was well-known in the last century as both a haven for migrating religious movements and a hotbed for faiths and cults of its own. "The Burned-over District" was the traditional nickname of this region, so swept by Protestant revivals that any flammable soul was presumed already charred or alight. Our twentieth-century forbears Arch Merrill and Carl Carmer pointed out "The Spirit Way," a long, narrow upstate stretch, roughly outlining I-90 from Albany to Buffalo, on which several important cults relocated or founded. We like the ring of the term, and so we'll use it. We noticed, however, that most of the religious-mystical activity they mentioned - as well as a lot more - took place in a smaller, more concentrated area than either of these, in a thirty-mile wide band slanting down from Rochester or thereabouts to the Southern Tier, right through the western half of the Western Door.

It could be said that the only way to tell a religion from a cult is the same way to tell a great book from a good: success two hundred years later. It's too early to judge all of those we find in these pages. Needless to say, though, the indispensable first quality of the would-be prophet (so many of whom we see on Spirit Way) is charisma, enough to attract followers. Sometimes this is a factor of such utter, unflinching self-belief - akin to, if not classifiable as, madness - that less certain natures gravitate around it. In other cases it may be rooted in simple canniness - "people-smarts" - and a persuasive personality. It may also be the sheer fact of stating religious truth. We do not know the all-hail hereafter so well that we claim to spot liars upon the subject, at least not until they have spotted themselves by their own hypocrisy.

One thing that impresses us curiously about many would-be theocrats is the sheer humility of their original goals. Some of them never seemed happier than during the brief periods when their lives had attained some stability. Most seem to have had above-average desires and below-average work ethic. The role of the prophet is a shortcut, but a hit-or-miss occupation. Most of those of the Spirit Way, we suggest, if offered early in their careers Achilles' choice, would have taken a comfortable middle-class existence - without undue effort, of course - over fitful glory.

It's a strange place, the Spirit Way, with a mercurial energy that makes for unlikely neighbors. The worst accounts of Jemima Wilkinson or Thomas Lake Harris read like those of Old World shysters Edward Kelley and Aleister Crowley. On the other hand, Handsome Lake and Father Baker, once they found their callings, were among the most altruistic people who ever lived. The ventures of Mordecai Noah and John Murray Spear were quirky, quixotic, and short-lived. Yet Joseph Smith and the Fox sisters (worthy tenants discussed in a different chapter) founded perhaps the two most influential modern religious movements in the world, coming to their great awakenings only a few miles apart.

We had originally intended a handy ten stories for this chapter, but decided that Lily Dale and the Chautauqua Institution were too obvious and well-known to need discussion. These two summer lake communities a few minutes' drive apart could be seen to represent differ-

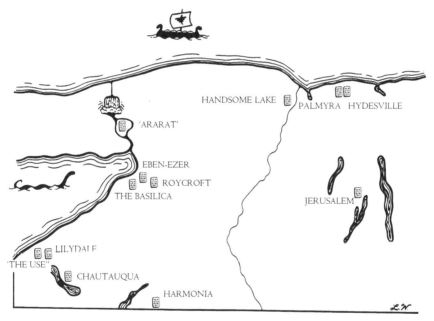

ing poles of outlook: Dionysus and Apollo, right-brain and left-brain, intuition and reason. (Chautauqua may not be able to forswear mysticism all the way to its roots, though, which were influenced by American Transcendentalism.) Both communities have been significant for a long time, almost as if some magic can be attributed to the sites themselves. Lily Dale's Cassadaga Lake is near burial mounds, even traces of an ancient graded road, and ossuaries - bone-fields - were found about the grounds of the Institution. We should merely need to mention their presence on Spirit Way - the holy "City of Light" of Spiritualism and the highbrow "Athens of the West" of enlightenment.

If we suggest Roycroft as another mystical community, our case for this small region should be made. Yet there were other inspired groups now largely forgotten but once sprouting by the virtual legion in the woods, valleys, and green rolling hills of the Western Door under the auspices of fire-eyed prophets. There has to be some energy here.

THE PUBLICK UNIVERSAL FRIEND

[The community of "the Jemimakins" lay along the shores of Seneca Lake, near Penn Yan and Jerusalem.]

There's not much debate about the facts of Jemima Wilkinson's life; it's in their interpretation that the rub lies. Some authorities speak from the evidence alone, presuming Jemima, at least much of the time, sincere. The most charitable view some of her episodes as inexplicable, possibly even paranormal. Others take the worst that was said of her for gospel, regarding every act of her adult life as a self-serving gesture aimed at gain. To them, "The Publick Universal Friend" was just another of the freaks of the Burned-over District.

Eighteen-year-old Jemima Wilkinson of Cumberland, Rhode Island, apparently died in 1776 of a plague. She was deathly still for several hours. At midnight she stood from her bed and spoke with a voice totally different... and inspired. It seemed that she'd undergone an out-of-body experience, and was now infused with the Spirit of "the Lord of Hosts" to show the sinners the new and revealed messages of God. Then she set to dinner with the appetite of an aerobic athlete.

Between the Sunday services at the Meeting House, Jemima drew the whole curious congregation off to a shady tree. In that time of marvels and frequent death, her neighbors praised the recovery; yet, no longer Jemima Wilkinson, it was all to be expected of "the Universal Friend of Mankind whom the mouth of the Lord hath named." The core of a sect was formed that walked half a century in her steps.

Jemima Wilkinson was an attractive woman with clear skin and glossy black hair. Her harshest critics presume chronic dislikes of work and above-average needs for prestige led to a career decision - her reception of the Holy Spirit. This is strong language; but in 1774 Jemima did attend meetings of a sect styled something like "The New-Lights." They were religious fanatics who claimed to live under the power and spirit of the Lord, receiving guidance and illumination from heavenly realms and attention and money from this one. Jemima may have noted.

As "The Publick Universal Friend" Jemima rode her rolling revival through Pennsylvania, southern New York, and Connecticut. Soon chiming along were her two apocalyptic witnesses, James Parker, channeling the Old Testament Elijah, and Sarah Richards, doing likewise for the prophet Daniel ("now operating in the female line"). They sound like early Spiritualists from here.

Jemima's peccadilloes along the path to her promised land are numerous and comical. Strung together they make her look like a Spirit-Way Curly, Larry and Moe rolled into one very affected female form. Exasperating, fleecing, and bankrupting would-be benefactors seemed all part of her pattern. "The Lord hath need," was her blithe reply to all protest. Money missing from a strongbox (after her stay with the state treasurer) miraculously appeared in her suitcases under search. She tried to con river porters of their fee for transporting her entourage to their destination, "The New Jerusalem." Even the tract they began to develop devolped a problem.

Jemima had suspected the land was vacant, or else counted on wheedling the "savages" out of it by persuading them she was an ambassador of the Great Spirit. She received an unhappy surprise. Messrs. Phelps and Gorham arrived claiming to own the land. Jemima had over 100 followers, however, and the two New Englanders were so eager to forward the settlement of the country that they arranged terms even pleasing to "the Lord."

Jemima's most comical misadventures involved her attempts to convert the Iroquois to Christianity and win herself lasting renown. She approached a Seneca council in a wood near Canandaigua and loosed her rant like a latter-day Moses. The Seneca listened in such total silence that she was sure her words had taken. They were simply astonished at her terrible manners. The Iroquois never interrupted anybody, even interrupters. They picked up and moved to another grove, resuming their talk as if nothing had happened.

Indignant but determined, Jemima tried again soon after. She charged up to a group of Oneida chiefs at Elmira and commenced her fire-and-brimstone as before, this time claiming to be their Savior. They listened, but she could read nothing from their reactions. At the end of her sermon one of the chiefs addressed her with a short speech in his own tongue. "The Friend" turned to an interpreter.

The chief had started by saying that the Iroquois had their own religion, which was doing them quite well. He'd added that someone rude enough to interrupt like that was in no position to give advice. Finally, he'd called Jemima Wilkinson an impostor, saying that if she were as great as Jesus Christ, she would need no translator to understand Iroquois words. Once convinced that the speech had registered, the Oneida presented their backsides en masse. Humiliated in front of her White disciples, The Friend set off for more gullible game.

In the "New Jerusalem" there was plenty of hard outdoor work for everyone else, but The Friend and her small coterie lived in luxurious style. Jemima even traveled about in a splendid coach with the letters "P. U. F." boldly blazoned on the sides. Nevertheless, here Jemima's pioneers could sip straight her fundamental and ascetic Christianity. (Jemima had developed at least a public dislike of sex. Before her religion days she had been in love with a young British officer; after his mortal meeting with a bullet in the Revolutionary War - and her transformation - she was affecting celibacy, like everyone else in the Friend's Jerusalem. In private, Jemima was allegedly more flexible. Word has it that she was interrupted in the close embraces of rich male benefactors more than once.)

Perhaps her flaws were by then evident to all, yet in her maturity, Jemima was honored and loved, a matriarch to her community. Even today the lore of the region features her frequent return, the spectral "Grey Lady," rescuing the lost. When in 1819 Jemima Wilkinson passed into that long rest for the second time - this one for good - two male parishioners disappeared into the woods with a white sheet wrapping the form she had left behind. Only natural monuments mark her secret peace, "The Publick Universal Friend."

THE CODE OF HANDSOME LAKE

[Initially many Iroquois were hostile to the Christian religion. Their own faith was dear to them, and many had been offended by some early missionaries, of whom one early writer could only wish that they "had been men of greater ability." Yet after the Revolution, the world was changing around the Six Nations so fast that the old faith was no longer keeping pace, and alcohol was causing deep divisions in Iroquois life. At the eighteenth century's end a new religion came to the Iroquois, the revelation of the famous "Handsome Lake" (*Ganeodiyo*, 1735-1815).]

Cornplanter's half-brother (by their Yankee father John O'Bail) was born on the banks of the Genesee near Rochester. Most of his life, it appears, Handsome Lake was too good a friend of John Barleycorn, and on the day that made his fame (the stories say), he had passed out in this association. His brothers found him dead on the ground. At his funeral in their house, Handsome Lake suddenly sat up and spoke. He held a big council of his people - to whom special dreams were important - and told all he'd seen in his sleep.

In Handsome Lake's vision (stripped of details), as he was looking out his window at the stars, expecting to die, three men so beautiful they had to be superhuman appeared and gave him berries to eat. This threw him into trance; they showed him many wonders, including the "Happy Hunting Grounds," the Iroquois heaven. They told Handsome Lake that he could return to the world if he would use his days to teach the will of the Great Spirit. He promised; they hurled him into sleep and disappeared. He woke, a changed man.

The Prophet gave the rest of his life to his vision from the Great Spirit. His doctrines did not replace the old rites so dear to the Iroquois; in fact, he advocated them. His code is as much morality guide as mystical treatise, with a Leatherstocking "Inferno" thrown in.

Hellish torments were meted to sinners: drunks drank boiling liquor; quarreling husbands and wives yelled till their eyes stuck out; abusive husbands hit red-hot statues (whose heat hit back!); the lazy did the labors of Sisyphus, tending gardens whose weeds regrew like Hydra-heads; sellers of land to Whites moved sand one grain at a time.

But many poetic gifts were given to those who kept the Great Spirit's laws, and the code of Handsome Lake contains his own commandments: morality, temperance, patience, forbearance, charity, forgiveness. But his most persistent sermons railed against "demon rum," which he saw destroying Iroquois society.

The Longhouse religion of Handsome Lake is still with the Six Nations and could serve as guides to people of all origins. The Prophet died at Onondaga in 1815, ever at work for his mission and his people.

NOAH AND THE NEW JERUSALEM

[For a long time artists, poets and even mystical outfits in the West had hankerings to recreate the old paradise of Eden or make themselves a new one. It was the rationale to many groups who drew off to the frontiers and formed settlements like those we encounter on Spirit Way. Furthermore, the temptation to give a Biblical interpretation to every phenomenon - even in the New World - was irresistible for many eighteenth- and nine-teenth-century folk. Accordingly, the Native Americans could be envisioned as descendants of the Lost Tribes of Israel; and Grand Island became, at least in one man's vision, the Promised Land.]

An article from *The Black Rock Gazette* of June 14, 1825 announced to the world that Grand Island - or most of it, anyway - had been sold. Two portions of it totaling two thousand acres had been purchased by Mister M. M. Noah of New York City. His purpose was nothing less than the resettlement of the Jews.

Mordecai Noah of New York City was editor of the National Advocate and, as the article stated, "a prominent Israelite." He was a large, muscular, congenial man, rather rotund. He was a councilor-at-law in our own courts and had held the important post of Consul General for the United States at Tunis. By the time of his Grand Island venture he had decided to found a great city where his oppressed brethren could live in peace. According to Noah the Native Americans were descendants of the Lost Tribe, and he planned also to bring them back into the Jewish fold. The Native Americans might have had their own ideas about this; but Grand Island - for reasons so far unclear to us - was selected as Noah's "City of Dreams."

Noah's published proclamation to the Jewish people announced that an asylum had been provided in a "fruitful and happy country" where their religion and their rights would be respected. It declared the Jewish nation reorganized under a government of Judges, ordered a census of Jews to be taken throughout the world, and directed foreign Jews to encourage emigration to his new province. The proclamation also ordered neutrality in the present war between Greece and Turkey, forbade polygamy, admitted that the Indians of this country were descendants of the Lost Tribes, and suggested "civilizing" them and teaching them their origins. It called for a tax of three silver shekels to be levied on all Jews to assist emi-grants, named commissioners to carry out the order, and was signed "by order of the Judge, A.B. Seixas, secretary pro tem."

Even those of his own faith foresaw disaster, but Mordecai Noah envisioned great commercial centers on Grand Island dominating the fron-tier. In August of 1825 he and A.B. Seixas, his enthusiastic assistant, packed their bags and insignia and left New York City for Buffalo and the new Israel.

If there was any trepidation about the prospect of a Jewish empire on the Niagara Frontier, one would not know it from the reaction of the locals. The scheme was welcomed with at least good-natured curiosity, and the fanfare of September 15, 1825 - the day the cornerstone was to be laid

- made open arms sound like a better description. Bells chimed, flags waved, artillery circled the Buffalo courthouse, and a great parade formed in front of the Masonic Lodge. Noah and his enterprise were rung in with a choreographed display involving marching bands, saluting soldiers, hearty speeches, solemn religious rites - Christian and Jewish - and a thundering cannon roar in honor of "The Twelve Tribes."

Grand Island was the projected site of the ceremonies, but as the day drew near, Noah worried about getting the whole parade over. Matters were relocated to St. Paul's Church in Buffalo. No one told the papers, however, and the shores of the Niagara near the island were lined with wagons filled with spectators, as well as cakes, beer, cold meats, fruit, and pies for sale.

The Buffalo parade involved representatives of Church and state, but it sounds like mostly a Masonic affair. Stewards bearing corn, wine, and oil joined the show, with Masonic potentates like the Principal Architect (with square, level, and plumb), and a Master Mason (with square and compass). "The Judge of Israel" - Noah himself - in fancy robes followed, and a passle of "Knights Templar" paced rear guard.

Noah addressed the assembly, announcing the reorganization of the Jewish government. He related in detail the history of the Hebrews - their sufferings, wanderings, and dispersion. The audience seemed impressed, listening with "profound attention." As the ceremonies ended, the procession marched back to the Masonic Lodge, and the militia went to the Eagle Tavern. Noah himself was back in New York in a day or so attending to further details. There were none.

Noah, his impractical proclamation, and his entire scheme were soundly denounced by prominent Rabbis throughout the world, and insults were hurled at his name. The dreamer for a time defended himself through the columns of his newspaper until the excitement waned.

The involvement of the Freemasons in Noah's Buffalo business is interesting, but hardly surprising. There has been a long and warm attachment between the Cabala - Judaic mysticism - and the secret societies of the west, among which the Masons must be listed.

We sense that there was quite a bit more to this Noah than meets the eye. Rumor holds that Noah was a Mason and had some very powerful patrons. (George Washington had attended his parents' wedding, and some feel that Noah's rise to prominence was suspiciously rapid.) We've heard through the grapevine that Noah stood for a Cabala-cult whose deep mystical tradition he hoped to make the constitution of the new order. It would only make sense.

One of the most interesting features of the Grand Island matter was the intended cornerstone of the new city of refuge, a rectangular, inscribed piece of sandstone. In mythological terms this might have served as a "world-navel" so familiar to students of the old religions. Most preindustrial cultures had some very terrestrial object - often a stone, a tree, or a bit of ground - to which they attached the most mystical of their thoughts. It's a significant gesture for a nineteenth-century Western man to be concerned with a stone like this. It almost implies some deeper source of wisdom behind this M. M. Noah, like the old mysticism the traditional societies are thought to preserve and not hand out for the asking.

The inscription on this stone began with a Hebrew line meaning, "Hear, O Israel, the Lord is our God - the Lord is one." In English, it was followed with:

ARARAT,
A city of Refuge for the Jews. Founded by
MORDECAI MANUEL NOAH
In the month of Tizri 5586 - Sept. 1825, in the 50th year
of American Independence.

Noah's corner stone, apparently forgotten against St. Paul's Church, was finally laid outside against the rear wall. Later someone moved it to Black Rock. In 1833 it made its way to Grand Island, and by 1850 the stone came to the Baxter Farm on the river shore about two miles above Whitehaven. By 1864 Noah's wandering rock was at Sheenwater, and, in two years more, had made its way to the Buffalo museum. It's with the Erie County Historical Society now.

THE STONE OF HELP

[West Seneca's Ebenezer Society was another of those curious communities that might have located itself anywhere but ended up here on Spirit Way. Four names are associated with the ideological roots of the Ebenezers, "The Community of True Inspiration": Johan Tauler (1300 - 1361), a fiery Dominican mystic; Thomas à Kempis (1380? - 1400), author of *The Imitation of Christ*, a classic of Christian mysticism; Jacob Boehme (1575 - 1624), long associated with the currents of European occult thought; and Philipp Spencer (1635 - 1705), more or less the founder of Pietism. The old records have little to suggest why the Ebenezers came to Western New York, but with that inspirational pedigree, how could they go elsewhere?]

Like many European squabbles, this one seemed over little, but religion was at its heart. According to some of its members the Lutheran Church was so far away from its roots that it had become corrupted, adopting "ritualistic form." By 1714, violent protest had broken out in the walled medieval cities of Germany. The dissenters - "The Community of True Inspiration" - had broken away.

With persecution their numbers grew. They withdrew from their society, refusing to take oath, to serve in the military, or to send their children to orthodox schools. They migrated to Hessen, a liberal German state, and took refuge in a walled, hilltop medieval castle. Their community declined as their comfort level grew, but in 1817 the visions of traveling tailor Michael Krausert led to a new revival. A wandering carpenter named Christian Metz took the group to the next logical step: a migration to a new land. On August 27, 1842, they assembled for their most solemn festival ("Liebesmahl"), where four men - among them Metz - were picked to seek settlement in America. Their voyage took thirty-seven days.

After surveying several tracts in the western region of New York State, they were enchanted by the parcel on the Seneca Reservation. Christian Metz called his fellows in the cult of "True Inspiration" to settle in this ancient wood, establishing the community of Eben-Ezer.

In their three villages - Upper, Lower, and Middle Eben-Ezer - these thrifty, hard-working folk prospered, largely through farming. By 1849 their settlements included a sawmill, a grist mill, a schoolhouse, a general store, a post office, homes, and of course, a church. The Ebenezers kept to themselves, however, which is probably well; a few of their traits would have unsettled their neighbors.

Foot-washing (straight out of the Bible) was part of Liebesmahl, their religious love feast. Like the Shakers, they shook when they were inspired by divine messages. Like the Perfectionists, they were stern in their criticisms of less-than-pious behavior. Like the Mormons, they were into a number of pre-Spiritualist occult practices that would have looked pretty anti-Christian: channeling, for instance. In each of their communities, one or several individuals served, for all practical purposes, as mediums.

They heard the Lord often in the woods and fields of the Spirit Way, but their mortal neighbors seem to have turned them off. By the later 1850's the Ebenezers wore out their welcome in Erie County with their harsh treatment of a young couple who had violated their marriage edicts. They were not granted an extension of their land charter, and, as the Civil War raged, the Lord called the thousand hardy souls to Iowa to build a new home called "Amana." Their descendants are there yet.

One curiosity remains, however. The name "Ebenezer" seems to mean "The Stone of Help." This term appears at times in association with the "Ark of the Covenant," that most mystical ancient Hebrew possession which, in its turn, has become occult shorthand for some unspecified source of wisdom and power, sought for centuries by individuals, societies and even nations - like Hitler's Nazis. Among the currents of mystical suspicion is the idea that the Ark may indeed be a physical object whose recovery - or its combination with other famous elemental treasures like the Holy Grail, the Spear of Destiny, and Excalibur - would guarantee great enlightenment, and, it would seem, vast power. These fabled treasures may also be code-concepts representing other objects; they may also be allegorical - ideas, secrets, moved about the globe with the descendants, lineal, mystical, or spiritual, of their last possessors. What was there in Western New York to attract so many Biblically-inspired people, interpreting Old and New Testaments in their own new ways? Is the Ark, whatever it is, here?

THE GOLDEN PLATES

[The story of the Church of the Latter Day Saints is surely too well known to need full summation here. What may surprise many people is the extent to which the early Mormons figure in American mystical folklore. We hope to show reasons to consider Joseph Smith (1805-1844) a founding tenant of the Spirit Way.]

This youngest son hiked among the wooded hills and still-mysterious stone ruins near his first home in central Vermont. His imagination must have fed. He was ten when his family - descendants of Revolutionary War soldiers - came to Western New York, a region swept in the early 1800's with fiery rhetoric and rival Protestant groups. It must have seemed then to Joseph Smith, as to any resident of the Burned-over District, that the path to all earthly glamor and moment lay in making public the private words of the Lord.

Five years later the spacey farm lad came in from the valley woods, pale and quaking after his first vision. In three years more, an angel clad in a robe of light came into his little bedroom in the Smith farmhouse. "Moroni" told a panoramic tale of prophecy, war, buried treasure, ancient American civilizations, and a book written in gold. Guided by this angel, on the night of the Fall Equinox in 1827 Joseph Smith found "the Golden Plates" in a cave in Palmyra's Hill Cumorah. Eleven witnesses testified to their existence. On the moonless night the tablets came from the ground, visions were widely reported in the region. Many people saw imposing, Classical-style armies marching across the sky amid light and percussion.

The tablets at first were incomprehensible, but with aids both animate (several scribes) and mineral (his mystical divining stones), Smith began dictating the Book of Mormon. (His two scrying-crystals the "Urim" and "Thummim" were set almost indescribably in the rims of a pair of giant otherworldly bifocals.) Before long, the Mormon Bible was in print, and the Church of the Latter-Day Saints beginning to form.

Smith's tale of the tablets was tragic and profound, a saga of the Lost Tribes of Israel populating the American continents. His book culminated in a civil war of which the prophet Moroni was the sole good survivor. The aboriginals encountered by Columbus, accordingly, were the survivors of this prehistoric conflict, and the book of Moroni their only coherent record.

Smith and his band of converts left the Spirit Way, moving westward from home to home. Though many urban Americans were deeply sympathetic to the Mormons' rights to practice their faith, they were persecuted in the rural regions they settled. They were not disposed to turn the cheek. They policed themselves with bands of religious hoods, and there were some violent battles within the faith. By the days of their Illinois settlement, Joseph Smith in a military uniform rode a white charger at the head of a five-thousand-man legion (which nearly came to civil war with the state militia). Assured of fair trial, Smith turned himself over in the summer of 1844; he was assassinated in a Carthage jail. It was decided that the budding faith would never win against such duplicity, and the move to Utah's Great Basin was made. The success of the Mormons is proverbial from there.

There's no archaeological support for either the Mormon tale in its whole or the idea that the Native Americans are transplanted Israelites. Yet a few things about Prophet Smith and the early Mormons make them interesting from occult vantages.

First off, many of the Prophet's gestures were those of the classic preindustrial mystic. He was a dowser, using his hazel rods to seek treasure and other buried items. He was prone to visions and practiced what we would call channeling. He carried a pair of small stones about with him, magic talismans that were all he was permitted to keep from the cache of precious, Classical-style objects he allegedly found buried on the west side of Cumorah Hill. (A variety of religious splinter groups less successful than the Mormons were also led by prophets with a penchant for burrowing into Native American earthworks. Some of the stones they wielded were doubtless ancient totems like Smith's.)

Joseph Smith was fascinated with the echelons and symbolism of the Masonic Order. Murdered Mason William Morgan's wife became one of Joseph Smith's several. Masonic ideology and hierarchical structure were used in forming the Mormon order. Indeed, Smith's final words ("O Lord My God..."), cut off by the rain of bullets, were the first of the Masonic distress cry.

It's likely that old mystical influences - like alchemy, hermeticism, and perhaps even ritual magic - arrived from late sixteenth-century Europe into early nineteenth-century Western New York and entered the development of Joseph Smith. John L. Brooke (*The Refiner's Fire*) traces the families of founding Mormons like Smith and Brigham Young back to their earliest New England roots, observing traditions of alchemy, herbal healing, and even witchcraft. In some cases Brooke traces the ships on which trunks of Old World "magical" texts crossed the Atlantic.

Though Mark Twain once referred to the Mormon Bible as "chloroform in print," it may be something more than that. Close analysis has found nothing to suggest that the text produced by Joseph Smith and company is literally authentic, but it's an impressive document for a man like Smith - even according to our revised impression - to have composed. It's heavier than simply a faked religious text cooked up by two or three people. At the very least the unconscious mind of Joseph Smith (if not his own psychic insights) was involved in the long production.

Occult scuttlebutt maintains that there was substantial mystical interchange between the Mormons and the Iroquois. High-placed Masons like Washington and Franklin were thought to have known about the golden tablets found by Joseph Smith; they were either given to the Six Nations for safekeeping, or had been in their possession all along. Some modern Iroquois claim their ancestors knew enough about Hill Cumorah to have left it strictly alone before the Mormon founder - perhaps led by his own strange angel - turned up the fateful plates.

HARMONIA

[The name "Kiantone" is from a Native American term meaning "planted fields," possibly referring to the ancient town whose traces have been found in this region south of Jamestown.]

The mystical roots were already deep when the Whites arrived. A mineral spring was a healing shrine to the Native Americans. No less than the mighty Cornplanter may have led his warriors to it before campaigns (like those of the seventeenth-century that won this territory for the Iroquois). By the middle of the nineteenth century those in Euroamerican mystical circles were well accustomed to thinking of the Southern Tier - especially Randolph and the Kiantone Valley - as a center of "the earth-force," possibly connected with the new phenomenon of electricity. The new religion, Spiritualism, found here a natural and ready home.

In 1852 public attention focussed on a spring in the area. Possibly the one so inspiring to Cornplanter, it filled many Whites with divine fire. This in itself is not unheard of: pools, fountains, and other inland sources of water have long been associated with saints and prophets; and conquering cultures (often forfeiting their own mystical tradition) often look for guidance to the conquered. What was curious was all that followed.

Shortly after the Fox sisters' 1848 rappings, the wife and daughter of blacksmith John Chase emerged from trance with the revelation that their Kiantone valley had once been inhabited by "the Kiantonians," a rich, sophisticated, and ancient race. A host of White mystics - including a New England Universalist minister - took up the cause.

Humanitarian, preacher, and Spiritualist medium John Murray Spear could have heard of the region and its spring from many sources; from then on he heard only those within him. "There would arise in a scene of natural beauty noble temples, great universities, and stately halls of art," said his voices, "all conceived in architecture of hitherto unknown beauty." Spear's eternal vision was of a model city based on universal brotherhood: Harmonia. A band of followers and a small campus of odd buildings soon materialized along the Kiantone Creek.

It should not surprise us that he was hard to stereotype, the Reverend John Murray Spear. Had he been one-dimensional he would not have led many people for very long. To some Spear was nothing other than a typical nineteenth-century fraud, a snake-oil salesman, Spiritualist-style. Others saw a multitalented man: an amateur scientist experimenting with electricity, a prophet, and an inspired poet. Still others saw the social pioneer whose ideas of government foreshadowed those of our own day, or the early feminist, the staunch and tireless campaigner for women's rights.

A New Englander named for the founder of the American Universalist church, Spear was a minister whose politics were too radical for his congregations. Sage and mighty spirits (evidently forming themselves into committees) had dictated guidance to Spear over a long period of time. They spoke through him, and others wrote. Their attention turned to community-building.

"The Association of Beneficents" - a band of spirits including Ben Franklin, Socrates, Thomas Jefferson, John Hancock, John Adams, Lafayette, Martin Luther, and Swedenborg - revealed a model social state. "The Educationizers" (led by Aristotle, Plato, and Jefferson again) contributed ideas about education and architecture. Spear's colonists dwelt in octagonal buildings, drank only water from springs certified as "magic," and lived by the dictates of Spear's spirit-guides. Seemingly a habit in some Spirit Way communities, they also gave up their possessions.

The citizens of Harmonia lived communally in multicolored cottages whose unusual shapes suggest sacred architecture. Willow trees (for a basket-weaving business) and berry bushes (for a money crop) were planted all over their ridge. Freedom in all things physical and spiritual was their practice, and this meant some unconventional ideas, for the day, about sex. (Part of this enlightened advice encouraged Spear to exchange his wife for a female secretary.)

In Spear's revelations, the site near the Kiantone Creek had first been inhabited by an ancient race of non-human critters who had left traces of their high civilization: a vast treasure, a source of mystical power, maybe even signs of their web-footed selves. Accordingly, the residents of Harmonia were at constant work, digging a strange tunnel into their hill. Wide enough for two people to walk abreast, it went back a hundred and fifty feet in a stairstep fashion.

To demonstrate their belief in freeing women from the "slavery of masculine control," the robed citizens of Harmonia held frequent festivals that featured midnight ceremonial marches emulating the Pope's Procession of Notice (but to their own cacophonous impro of bells, horns and tin pans). One of them in the late 1850's roused so much curiosity that more than five thousand people attended.

While some visitors came to the warm, moonlit hill to hear the speaking of the spirits, others were full of their own liquid ones and up for a spectacle. During a trance-session describing the sexual freedom of the community, a voluptuous Cattaraugus maid contorted herself seductively, and at one point moaned, "Free Love is God's Law!" We're unsure whether the ensuing tumult was due to righteous Victorian males and females expressing their outrage at the "obscenity," or repressed ones too-suddenly enlightened, and trying to get at each other. Although a riot was averted by "the magnetic and persuasive oratory" of Kiantone resident Mrs. Britt, the episode began the slide of Harmonia.

We should not need to say that neither treasure nor frog-footers ever materialized, but one aspect of the Harmonia community has people still shaking their heads. Guided by the channeled words of Ben Franklin, a spiritual sub-group of the Harmonians (called "The Electricizers") built a mysterious machine - "a living organism, quickened by an indwelling spiritual principle." Of course the whole idea sounds bogus; but those who saw this contrivance have not described an ordinary machine. It sounds a bit like an eternal motion machine and a bit like Frankenstein, with a dose of alchemy swirled in. A mob believed enough in its validity to storm its quarters and destroy it.

In 1858 the great convention of the Kiantone Community had made the New York City papers, but only the faithful had ever sensed the mystical energy that drew them, and even that seems to have faded by 1870. Spear was off to other ventures, leaving the rainbow campus to decompose slowly across the next century. The willows and berry bushes are all that remain, troubling the modern residents attempting to put the land about them to use.

Though they enjoyed the sublime parlor-games and sometimes even profited from the enterprise, most Spiritualists were wary of taking the spooks too literally, usually venturing little upon their sayso. John Murray Spear put all he had on them, pursuing his visions as long as we can track him. Nevertheless, from our perspective the Kiantone community was one of the wackier tenants of the Spirit Way.

THE BROTHERHOOD OF THE NEW LIFE

The lakeshore folk were becoming suspicious. In the spring of 1868 a man from downstate spent a quarter of a million dollars buying up 2,000 acres of prime Portland farmland. Soon a pretty group of ladies and gentlemen arrived for some pretty hard work: tending land, developing vineyards, establishing a winery, and laboring for spiritual advancement. This was the inspired community of Thomas Lake Harris - "The Brotherhood of the New Life" - moving into their third site.

Harris (1823-1906) was a former minister who had taken up community-building under a likely gumbo of mid-nineteenth century influences: American Transcendentalism, the Universalist church, and the inspired musings of two famous psychics, Swedish mystic Swedenborg and American healer Andrew Jackson Davis. Harris had grown up in Utica, NY, and, before his community-building days, had been active in the budding movement that would soon be called Spiritualism, collaborating on a magazine of esoterica called *Univercoelum*. He and Edgar Allan Poe may have been influenced heavily by one of Andrew Jackson Davis' 1840's trances. (Davis - a founding father of American Spiritualism - was impressive.)

Possibly under the influence of the apocalyptic Millerite movement (another Spirit Way group we may address someday), Harris founded his first community in Virginia. He set up his own Swedenborgian church in New York, where his congregation included Henry James (father of author Henry and parapsychologist William) and Horace Greeley, Utopian socialist and patron of the Fox sisters. This roundabout course eventually led him to the Spirit Way.

The Brocton group held up to a hundred men, women, and children, most of them high rollers, all seeking spiritual perfection. Only an exceptional person could have made these international lords and ladies trade their comfortable lives for hard labor and communal living. Thomas Lake Harris had amazing charisma.

Harris did not fit the image of the egalitarian Spiritualist. He had a monopoly on the spirit-talking in his community, and, upon joining it, the brothers and sisters of the New Life forfeited all the possessions of their old lives - land, houses, money, jewelry - to Harris. Like another legendary tempter who comes to mind, Harris could play hard-to-get until his game was chasing him. His rich devotees virtually begged him to accept their worldly goods and give them The Answer. Yet Harris, the evidence suggests, was more than a simple fake.

Harris became the most prominent of the "trance poets" of his day, ad libbing better poetry with his eyes closed than many poets write with paper, pen, and time. He dictated rhymed verse nonstop for hours, delivering even epic-length poems in only a dozen sessions. His visions taught him about humankind, the heavens, and the dawning of the New

Age. Most of the pace of dictation, rapid as it was, was dictated by the limits of the various secretaries, who surely suffered writer's cramp anyway. The best stretches of Harris' poetry look like the juvenilia of Shelley, or like rejected verses from "Prometheus Unbound": cosmic, platonic, and watery.

Another curiosity that could only have tested the members of "The Use" (as the Brotherhood was known to its residents) was Harris' preoccupation with new names. These were spiritually divined by "The Faithful" (as Harris preferred to be titled), and seem designed to bait some members and con others. The willful and macho Laurence Oliphant could hardly have enjoyed toiling under the new sobriquet "Woodbine," though a female who seems to have caught Harris' eye might not have cooled to be called "Golden Rose."

For many of us, Harris' peculiar expertise in separating people from their money is what stands out. Some of his followers were very generous: Jane Lee Waring, Harris' secretary and third earthly wife, gave over a quarter-million dollars. An Englishwoman donated $100,000, though her son was the more famous convert: journalist, traveler, diplomat, member of the House of Commons and man of the world Laurence Oliphant, whose trade of London's high living for Brocton's labor gave The Use instant legitimacy.

Oliphant (1829-1888) was the rage of London in a gentlemanly sense, an aristocratic Scot with religious parents. Before becoming Member of Parliament in 1865 he'd been an adviser to several Prime Ministers, and had several good careers (even adventures in international intrigue). He sounds like a real swashbuckler.

Hard was his Brocton labor, but hard, too, must have been Oliphant's separation from his lovely new bride, Alice LeStrange. ("I am an ardent lover," one of his letters moaned.) They married in 1872 and came to the community, but could not live together. Brother Thomas ministered to every aspect of his disciples' lives. Soon her significant wealth too became his. (We can imagine "Woodbine" boiling as he toiled.)

It's not easy to summarize Harris' beliefs, though he left thousands of pages of explanation. One thing is certain: the religion was run by Harris, who, in trance, communed with the "unseen ministers" of our realm and the beings who resided in the heavenly ones. In general Harris followed the pattern of his influences, largely Swedenborgian and Spiritualist. Themes of purity, spiritual ascension, and life as "a vale of tears" (from which we can communicate with the realm beyond) would have been quite familiar to 1990's New Agers.

Harris had a few new wrinkles. He taught practices of "Divine Respiration" - precise breathing - that could help one experience the spiritual plane on earth. This may seem an odd idea, but it's quite in keeping with old tradition (and not all that different from the ideas of the soon-to-come Gurdjieff in Europe). Many world cultures - Egyptian, Greek, Hindu, and Chinese - put heavy significance into breath, thinking

it connected to the life-force; and many old words for soul or spirit - ka, pneuma, prana, ch'i - mean or involve breath.

Another of Harris' notions would ensure him a dubious fame: his doctrine of "heavenly counterparts," in which each individual has "a spiritual lover," a soul-mate on the ethereal plane just for him or her. The union of perfect mates was apparent, too, in Harris' term for the Ultimate Being, "The Two-In-One." Harris let on not only that he had united with his spirit's mate, but that she was as much a celestial aristocrat as he an earthly one - the marvelous Queen Lily, his heavenly wife, on whom he fathered two cherubs. This apparent act of ethereal bigamy seemed not to ruffle his mortal family - a wife and two sons.

Not surprisingly, at about this point in the philosophy the matter turns to another subject common in counterculture cults, sex (of which there was little for anybody but Harris). Other members of the Brotherhood labored toward similar revelation and union, but while living (so far as Harris could ensure it) in earthly celibacy. Those who were still too emotionally earthbound to be able to see the way - always, in Soul-Doctor Harris' diagnosis, attractive females - might jump-start their spirit-progress another way: through Harris' close evening embrace.

We have no basis for judging Harris' success in heavenly terms, but in earthly ones, he could have done far worse. In some form and location the Brotherhood thrived almost forty years (1861-1900), during which a major source of income was the wine made and sold by its members. Harris, his philosophy, and his community were prime Spirit Way players for a good while, influential worldwide far longer.

Toward the end of its Brocton stay (in the early 1880's), one of the Brotherhood's most distinguished members had a few ideas of his own about the "New Life." Englishman Oliphant came to resent Harris' micromanagement of everyone's lives - and finances. He sued Harris for return of his "investment" in the New Life, which he eventually won. As things were heating up in Brocton, Harris heard the call to a new community. He and Jane Lee Waring founded another wine and-respiration-based collective near Santa Rosa, California.

Harris' last years were spent in Florida, California, and New York. At 83 he died, leaving followers so convinced of his resurrection that they waited days for it. They let him be buried only after the ashes and dust that had come together as Thomas Lake Harris gave unmistakable notice of their reversion back.

A community member eventually took over the Brocton site, which became a forerunner of the vineyard business so famous in the lakeshore region. The mansion "Vinecliff" and the rest of the curious buildings survive yet in good shape.

Yet there was a pathetic side to Harris' doings, and for us this incriminates his entire undertaking. Members of The Use endured great and useless suffering, "purifying their spirits" through fasting and ceaseless labor, much of it outdoors in the Western New York elements. (Laurence Oliphant suffered frostbite during nocturnal labor in a roaring storm, and his old mother did endless stitching with her arthritic fingers.) Harris was shamefully cold to members who had given their lives to him and then begun to wonder. One can only imagine the sentiments of the aging Lady Oliphant, sick with cancer, who'd followed Harris to his new home in California to confront him with her staggering faith; a ring on the finger of the callous guru's new bride was one Lady Oliphant's late husband had given to her. The hollowness of her prophet must have seemed to invalidate her whole life. She died with these feelings six days later.

THE LACKAWANNA SAINT

[We should not forget that the energy of Spirit Way manifests itself in mainstream faiths as well.]

Father Nelson Henry Baker (1841-1936) is known as the force behind Lackawanna's magnificent Our Lady of Victory Basilica; but his most meaningful monuments may have been in the lives of perishing humans. At his death the Buffalo Times wrote:

To the hungry during his ministry he fed fifty million meals. During the Depression at one time he was serving more than a million meals a year. He gave away a million loaves of bread. He clothed the naked to the number of a half million. He gave medical care to 250,000 and supplied medicines to 200,000 more. Three hundred thousand men, women, and children received some sort of education or training at his hands. A hundred thousand boys were trained for trades. Six hundred unmarried mothers in their distress knocked at his door and did not knock in vain. More than 6,000 destitute and abandoned babies were placed in foster homes... Men will give thanks that he lived and bless his memory.

One of the greatest humanitarians who ever lived was born on the East Side of Buffalo in February 1841. Like many classic saints, the second son of Lewis and Caroline Donnellan Baker seems to have shown no early signs of his priestly calling. He served in the New York State militia during the Civil War and in business after. By 1868 the soon-to-be Father started Latin lessons, and entered the seminary a year later. He toiled faithfully with humble flocks for a few years; yet one of his colleagues from these early days wrote that there was something a little special about this Baker fellow, and the notion of "miracles" came up. Folklore perpetuates itself in familiar patterns, into which, not surprisingly, the Father Baker legends fall.

Locks of his hair, pieces of his clothing, and rosaries and medals merely touched by Father Baker were said to cause healings. The lame walked, the ill recovered, and even the dead (or near-dead) revived, all at the good Father's touch or prayer. Even multiplication - one of Jesus' traditional miracles - is ascribed to Father Baker. (In every tale he sees personally to the handing-out of food and other scarce items at vast gatherings for the needy. They never run short.)

Baker gave so much away that he always lacked, and many of his miracles are associated with simply finding money to continue his work. Tales of miraculous gifts are similar to Old World fairy lore. Bills the Father could not pay were left under a statue of Our Lady; in the morning the exact fee was found on top of them. Once after he gave away his last dollar, someone walked up and handed him a twenty. After prayer when Father Baker was in desperate need, a stranger brushed him and put an envelope of money in his pocket. Even the well-known "Vanishing Hitchhiker" gets into the act. (We should all have one like this: silent and muffled under hat, collar, and scarf, he left an envelope with $2,500 on the back seat.)

In some tales the august Father even embodies the Trickster of the American Southwest, familiar virtually worldwide. In this motif, the Father faces some situation - say, crushing taxes on the marble imported for his Basilica - and finds a genial solution. (His chatting distracts the taxman; the marble's unloaded and Basilica-bound before anyone's wise.) [Like classic sacred sites, the Basilica was designed by an expert in "ecclesiastical (sacred) architecture" (Emile Ulrich).]

Religious figures in many cultures are associated with springs and wells. The Renaissance-style Basilica will forever be linked to the natural gas that since 1891 has supplied fuel to the OLV institutions. Inspired by a vision of Our Lady herself, Father Baker led a procession to the very spot, buried an image of Our Lady, and told the workmen where to drill. Expense and discouragement followed, but gas was found at 1,137 feet, a remarkable depth. Some consider Father Baker unique for exploiting this miraculous well (though that might be news for the Delphic Oracle). At the very least he was a rare dowser.

A boat trip with Father Baker revealed his power over weather. A storm rose up; a boat towing many sisters began to sink. The Father prayed and distributed medals; the storm subsided, and rescue came. Like many classic saints, Father Baker was even said to have been visited by Satan. We know no more of the story, but doubt not that the Arch-Deceiver was handed his walking papers directly.

Miracles surround Father Baker's death: bleeding crucifixes and visions of Our Lady of Victory. (The crucifix is still occasionally shown, with stains, to visitors.) Many still make pilgrimages to his grave and pray to him along with St. Jude in hopeless cases. Angels - or somebody - have been reported playing the basilica organ at night. We've heard reports that paranormal events still occur.

When his life's work was done, Father Baker's will revealed that this man who had handled millions in his ninety-five years was an utter pauper; he had given it all away. Baker may eventually be sainted by the Church, among whose considerations for such an honor miracles fall; yet it still astonishes us to hear such tales of an urban figure in a modern country. And here's a natural miracle, maybe the most eloquent of all: as Father Baker lay in state, so many thousands passing touched his hands that the gloves on them were worn through.

THE STORYTELLER'S BAG

The sorcerer is a much less dangerous person than the magician: the former might be described as a primitive scientist, whereas the latter, the true witch, is a compulsive ill-wisher and ill-doer.

Peter Partner

THE KEEPERS OF THE WESTERN DOOR

In 1609 on the west bank of the lake named for him, French explorer Samuel de Champlain had the White world's first encounter with the Iroquois (symbolically, a violent one). Alongside their Huron and Algonquin enemies, Champlain made no good first impression. Hostilities commenced, and at the first blast of his gun, three Iroquois fell dead, including two chiefs. The Iroquois (probably Mohawks) scattered, but the French had taken a position that was to curse them for centuries. Even in 1687 they thought the fearless Confederacy could be impressed by arms. The Marquis de Denonville landed at Irondequoit (near Rochester) and launched a ruinous attack against a big Seneca town. Within a year the Iroquois lashed back into Canada and repaid the French tenfold, causing at least a thousand deaths and driving the colony to the edge of collapse. Continued French blunders with the Iroquois Confederacy helped lose the continent to the English.

The people we have long called the Iroquois call themselves *Hodenausaunee*, "People of the Long House." The French, who knew of them first from their Algonquin enemies, give us our familiar name for them, *Iroquois* (from an Algonquin snicker meaning something like "real snakes"). It may have been an indignant term, but it was a respectful one, and another might confuse some readers. The Six Nations folk still seem comfortable calling themselves *Iroquois,* so we'll use it, at least until we become aware that the situation has changed.

The origins of the Iroquois are still debated. Though some feel they may have been medieval immigrants to upstate New York, many suspect that their ancestors had been here thousands of years, but had become culturally distinct only a few centuries before Columbus arrived. By the middle of the fifteenth century the Iroquois were a handful of upstate nations whose language was similar to that of their Huron foes. The Iroquois were hunters, farmers, and warriors. Their greatest arts were poetry, storytelling, and oratory. It was in the latter capacity that the Six Nations so impressed the White world.

In the middle of the sixteenth century a man named *Deganoweda* ("The Master of Things," sometimes called "The Peacemaker") brought together the five culturally and linguistically similar nations (the Cayuga, the Mohawk, the Oneida, the Onondaga, and the Seneca) into the Iroquois Confederacy, a single union called "The Five Nations." This band of gifted, warlike nations was within a century the strongest native power on the continent. (In the early eighteenth century another related nation of emigrants from the south, the Tuscarora, were taken into the confederacy, forever more called "The Six Nations.") Though the Confederacy was never a numerous body by the standards of the Old World (or those of Central and South America) it had an impressive form of representative government that many believe was used as an outline for the young United States.

The Seneca (the Six Nations people whose traditional territory was our survey area) are another group whose historic name is not their own. Since in the Seneca's origin-myth they came from the hill at the top of Canandaigua Lake, they called themselves *Nundawaono*, meaning "People of the Great Hill." The name that comes to us through the Dutch and English as *Seneca* (like the Roman playwright) is probably a corruption of a willful Algonquin misunderstanding (*a'sinnaker*) of their own name, which, naturally, came out bitter: "standing stones."

The Seneca were the largest and most warlike of the Iroquois nations. These "Keepers of the Western Door" were the defenders of the western entrance to the great landscape-long house of the Six Nations territory; they were the wardens of the most likely route of attack from their Native American rivals. How ironic that their greatest threat came from the other direction. How tragic its result.

As the most powerful and organized Native American body in the northeast, the Iroquois were prime players in a political sense, and possibly others. Some factions of the occult underground maintain that the founding fathers, steeped in Masonic lore, may even have conferred mystically with the Iroquois. Franklin and Washington are rumored of initiation into Six Nations mysteries. This may just be scuttlebutt. It may also be one of those tidbits of history that people uninterested in supernaturalism in any sense let lapse into the dustbin.

Some of our stories about famous Iroquois (Red Jacket, Cornplanter, and, in a later chapter, Joseph Brant) contain more words of biographical discussion than metaphysical, and to readers interested only in paranormal spills and thrills this may seem padding. Far from it; rather, we felt that the stories of these people were so interesting and charismatic apart from their mystical-paranormal associations that the opportunity to retell them (and perhaps interest others) was priceless. Maybe it's the old teacher coming out in us, always looking for a "hook" to draw students into learning something meaningful before they realize it isn't supposed to be fun. We admire them, these "People of the Long House." Enjoy our look at their supernatural history.

IROQUOIS WITCHES

The Iroquois had a powerful belief in witchcraft. They feared it, they hated it, and they killed anyone convicted of practicing it quickly. Anyone (man, woman, child, even animal) could be a witch, though it seems that the women took it on the chin too much of the time. More recently, accusations of witchcraft were used to get rid of political opponents and undesirables. Yet mainstream Iroquois religious ritual (like that of practically all old cultures) looks like magic to most modern Americans. What distinguished witchcraft from religion (or good magic) is another question.

In old Europe there were two general styles of magic. One was more or less the Egyptian-Greek tradition of "natural magic." (The mage manipulated natural forces to do his or her business, like diverting a stream to water fields.) In the other form (rooted in the Hebrew-Middle Eastern tradition of "angel-magic") the mage appealed to a spook to do the diverting. (Trouble comes in that the spook usually wants something back.) It might be that the type of magic Iroquois society resented was the second kind.

However, in many world cultures some form of proscribed religion operated in the shadow of the mainstream. It was often vigorously persecuted. The Iroquois seem to have had their own devil, "The Evil-Minded One," and it could be argued that their witches were his devotees. Otherwise, though, witches might just have been people who used magic to hurt. Healers were people who used it to help.

Sometimes people were made witches with the aid of others; an initiation would seem part of the process, and a brew that, when ingested, finishes the trick. One of the traditional powers of the Iroquois witch (like the Celtic druid) was shape-shifting: the ability to become another being, usually an animal, and still think as a human. (This, of course, is connected to shamanism, a type of religious expression found in all parts of the world.) The Iroquois have many stories of witches becoming animals, often farm critters or pets: dogs, horses, cats, or pigs. In these forms they do malicious damage to their human enemies and suffer injuries from whips, gunshots, and accidents. The animals flee, and their human forms have analogous wounds. This is also an Old World motif.

(Cephas Hill gave a tale to Carl Carmer: Once, in his boyhood, strange pigs were heard squealing in the shed of a Seneca who had just died. An old woman said they might be witches, and young Hill gave them both barrels of his shotgun. They fled, and the next day some children told him they saw a man by an abandoned cabin picking buckshot out of his backside. "Witch!" they cheeped, and he ran.)

For those suffering the effects of spellcraft, Arthur Parker (*The Code of Handsome Lake*) describes a deliciously sinister ceremony involving the heart of a black bird (a crow will do) hung by its chords over a lonely fire at night in the deep woods. Toast it slowly. Whoever's witching you will show up in a spectral form in the leaves above you and at least tell you why. If you really mean business, let it burn all the way. They'll be dead when they're found in the morning.

Sometimes a witch will work through a little object (a splinter, a piece of bone) somehow placed in the body of the victim. Burning this will do the job; the job is finding it. When Jesse Cornplanter returned from World War I a family on another reservation had some hard feelings for him. He didn't know how hard till he got sick. He lost weight and couldn't eat. White doctors hadn't been much help. In recollection he chuckled to Carl Carmer, "I was almost tasting strawberries" (such as line the Iroquois heaven-road), an Iroquois way to say "pushing up daisies."

One of the old men of the reservation said he had been witched. On four mornings the fellow gave him an emetic (made of touchwood fungus) and twelve quarts of water to drink. He vomited many times into a hole the old man dug in the ground. On the fourth day, up came a little sliver of wood. They built a fire, burned some tobacco over it, and threw in the thing to turn the spell around. Jesse Cornplanter learned just a short time later that the woman he suspected of hexing him had died. He was sorry, but it was her life or his.

THE TRIAL OF RED JACKET

In 1795 the French Duke de Liancourt, touring the frontier, expressed his desire to see Red Jacket (*Sagoyewata*, 1750-1830), the famous orator of the Senecas. His traveling companions told him he already had, several miles back: one of the figures sleeping off a drunk in a ditch along the trail at Avon.

Rhetoric was one of the transcendent arts of the Six Nations. Their speechmakers were world-renowned in their day, and the man we call Red Jacket was one of their greatest. His Iroquois name means something like, "He can't shut up," so it appears that even his word-wizardry could be tiring. Red Jacket's familiar name was likely due to his fondness for a British soldier's coat, but he was even fonder of a broad silver medal given him by George Washington (sort of a patron saint to the Six Nations and the only White man allowed in their heaven).

Someone who lacked modern insights once called Red Jacket "a rude and unlettered son of the forest," but the same observer thought his intellectual powers were unsurpassed. "His talents," said Captain Horatio Jones, the well known interpreter and "Indian" agent, "were among the noblest that nature ever conferred," ranking him with the Greek and Roman orators. Others simply called Red Jacket the greatest man who ever lived. (He was not, however, a warrior; this was a curiosity among the Seneca. Joseph Brant called him "Cow Killer.")

In many a learned argument, Red Jacket seems to have foiled the White authorities. His eye was said to be the most expressive in nature, and his scorn (besting some sanctimonious bureaucrat or clergyman with a rich phrase) probably had to be seen to be imagined. It was Red Jacket who said to a priest: "If you White people murdered your Savior, make up for it yourselves. We would have treated him better." It was he who, observing Whites build a bridge, walked away shaking his head, first muttering the phrase, "Damn Yankees." Outside the Batavia courthouse (after a tragic trial in which an Iroquois was sent to prison for stealing some minor items from Joseph Ellicott's home), someone pointed out to Red Jacket that a statue represented Justice. "Where is he now?" he replied.

In the spring of 1821 one of Red Jacket's fellow Seneca died in strange circumstances. Witchcraft was suspected, and blame fell on the woman who'd cared for him during his illness. After some consideration she was condemned to die. A chief was appointed to carry out the execution, but at the critical moment he choked - perhaps at the power of the witch - and it was left to a chief named *Soonongise* (commonly called "Tom Jemmy") to act. (Other aspects of this case we discuss more fully in "The Old Main Street Cemetery.")

The Whites of the region were angered and horrified. The authorities threw Tom Jemmy into jail. At his trial, Red Jacket came to the stand, and after taking about all the scolding he needed from the prosecutor, thundered a little lightning of his own. He argued that the Seneca were a sovereign nation, that the execution was not illegal according to their laws, and that, anyway, the imprisoned chieftain was just the executor of the decision. When the prosecutor and others sneered at the Iroquois belief in witchcraft, it was all the great speechmaker needed.

"Go to Salem!" he raged. "Your black-coats stormed the same doctrine from the pulpits, your judges pronounced it from the bench, and now you would punish our brother for adhering to the faith of his fathers and of yours! Go to Salem," he finished, recalling that pungent legacy then not much over a century old. Then he reminded the courtroom of the White treatment of the Son of God, their own savior, eighteen centuries before that. Whether persuaded or merely buffaloed, the Supreme Court let the prisoner go.

To some Europeans and colonials, the susceptibility to alcohol was a character failing, and the stodgiest old timers demean Red Jacket for his troubles in this regard. (This was one sense in which Washington's bright medal did him no favors: it made Red Jacket the only Native American of his day able to drink in a tavern.) Yet distilled spirits did not exist in either American continent before the Europeans brought them, and the Native Americans are no more to be blamed for this failing (to the extent it truly existed) than for an inability to resist smallpox.

Red Jacket (who "died exulting that the Great Spirit had made him an Indian") was originally buried in the Old Indian Graveyard at Buffum Street in Buffalo, but his remains were moved in the late 1800's to Forest Lawn, where a fine statue of him stands. Yet the association of Red Jacket and witchcraft does not end with the story we have just told, and it involves another famous Seneca - Cornplanter.

CORNPLANTER'S ACCUSATION

Though Cornplanter (*Garyanwaga*, 1736-1836) was half-White (the son of a colonial trader by a Seneca maid), his war-skills and wood-craft made him a chief. During the frontier wars Cornplanter's name ranked with those of Joseph Brant and the loyalist Ranger Walter Butler, striking terror in the White settlers. He was probably with those two at the infamous massacre of Cherry Valley.

Cornplanter also struck against those of his own color, however, in the Southern Tier, in the Alleganies, wiping out whole villages, even nations, that dared to stand against Iroquois aspiration. Cornplanter even captured his own father John O'Bail during a wartime raid in 1779. By way of family introduction, Cornplanter boasted of the scalps he had taken and the prisoners he had tortured to death. He then released his father with an escort and gifts.

Martial speeches were not the only ones Cornplanter could deliver. In 1790 before George Washington, Cornplanter nobly articulated the Native American confusion at their treatment by the warring European powers. As might be imagined, the Native Americans (making their decisions upon premises of honor) had little perspective of Euroamerican politics.

Partly under Cornplanter's leadership, the Seneca had backed the losing side (first the French and then the English) in two successive eighteenth-century wars. His influence suffered badly in the aftermath. Cornplanter also had a hand in land sales to the White settlers - and the needle-tongue and dagger-wit of Red Jacket were letting no one forget. Some besides Cornplanter were probably jealous of the honors Red Jacket had received. George Washington's bright medal was on his chest for all to see, and everyone knew he had addressed the Congress. Thus by the end of the eighteenth century Cornplanter had reasons to make some kind of move - and allies if it were against Red Jacket.

Possibly with the aid of his brother Handsome Lake (before his revelation), Cornplanter had the great orator charged with spitting fire at night or some other deed of the like that spelled witchcraft. Many details are lost to us; but this was a serious, even capital, offense. It was not, however, Red Jacket's first brush with either witchcraft or litigation. For three hours at his trial he hectored the Iroquois, and a majority voted in his favor. Cornplanter's political fortunes swooned, and seem never to have recovered.

After his debacle with Red Jacket, Cornplanter returned to his land in the Southern Tier. He seems to have devoted his life to improving the lot of his own folk, and advocated the adoption of agriculture and many other European practices. He became a tribal historian and a great storyteller, and he had another encounter with witchcraft.

Cornplanter's daughter Jiiwi took sick in 1800 after giving birth. The Senecas (led again by Handsome Lake) accused some unnamed

Delawares of conspiring to kill Jiiwi through witchcraft to spare the child's Delaware father "Silver Heels" (John Logan) "the responsibility of matrimony." This was probably the result of tension from the forced relocation of some Delawares (traditional Iroquois enemies) to the region of the Southern Tier. Things quickly got out of hand.

Cornplanter's entire Seneca band seemed ready for a war that nearly broke out in Chautauqua, Erie, and Warren (PA) counties, then with sparse White populations. Militia and negotiators were called in from as far away as Ohio and Canada, and a report was sent to the Secretary of War. Fortunately the matter cooled.

In old age Cornplanter offered his services to the United States in the War of 1812. This was gratefully declined, but his own son led a body of Seneca volunteers like the one that, half a century later, would be accounted "the finest company in the (Union) Army." Near the end of his life, Cornplanter had a very strong dream. He followed the Iroquois custom, wandering from house to house seeking someone to explain it. On the third day, he found an insight that made sense.

"You've been a chief too long," he was told. "You must appoint your successor. And if you wish to please the Great Spirit, get rid of everything made by the White man." Cornplanter gathered all his gifts from various Presidents, among which were a military uniform, a sword, and a medal. He burned them solemnly, staring into the embers of the fire until all were ruined. His tomahawk he sent to the man who succeeded him.

In 1836 near the age of one hundred Cornplanter passed to his next life. He was buried on his own land at the foot of an inspiring tree. As the old warrior and poet would probably have wished, its sweeping branches were his only monument.

THE STONE GIANTS

[Many cultures have legends of a tribe of monstrous opponents with which their forbears battled. Some would interpret these tales as ancestral memories of a prehistoric quarrel.]

The Iroquois called them "the Stone Giants." Fearsome in character and appearance, they seem to be flesh and blood. Even the Shawnee have legends about them, named for their hard armor or outer skins, weapon-proof scales gained by rolling in sand. The Iroquois' Algonquin enemies believed their own *wendigo* acquired his stony protection that way, too.

Originally the Stone Giants were a neighboring tribe content to live and let live, but in their wanderings they endured famine in the cold of the north. They turned to raw flesh for sustenance, and came back into Iroquois territory with a taste for fresh Homo sapiens - as may be imagined, a source of intercultural discomfort. It seems as if the then-Five Nations, doughty fighters though they were, were getting the worst of the business and nearing a precarious state. It was then that the tide turned, and there are two versions of the matter.

In one, an Iroquois warrior who'd grown from an impressionable boy into a bold and mighty young man (the famous "Skunny-Wundy") vowed to rid his nation of the trolls. He made a legend for himself among his own people, but his fame was not yet supernatural when he returned to his belongings on the bank of a creek and encountered one of the Stone Giants. A woman of this magical tribe inspected his tomahawk. She tasted it, licking the edge with her tongue, and then set about to see what it could do. The weapon shocked her by splitting a boulder at just a touch.

Unaware that it was her own act - her saliva - that (in the language of myth) gave the weapon some of the horrific magic that protected her tribe, the Stone Giantess presumed the weapon's owner was a warrior mighty enough to best her whole nation. The Iroquois hero was in no hurry to correct her, and added that he'd give her folk some of the boulder's medicine if they ever troubled his people again.

In another version of the Stone Giants' demise, the creator-god of the Six Nations disguised himself as a studly specimen of Stone Gianthood and persuaded his new colleagues to gather against the Five Nations into a single army. They camped at the god's direction in a valley into which he started an avalanche from above. The Stone Giants were overwhelmed, but one got away, setting up shop in the Alleganies (near High Hat and modern Bigfoot sightings).

THE OWL CAP

[In 1937 Jesse Cornplanter claimed that this tale was given him by an aged, toothless storyteller.]

In the old days, an orphan boy lived with his grandmother at the edge of the village. He was a good, helpful lad, but people had their doubts about her. He was five or six when he realized that every night she went out into the woods. She prodded him to see if he was asleep, then when satisfied went up into the loft and rustled around. He always heard a strange noise, and then she was gone. She came back late, chuckling softly to herself.

The orphan wondered very much what was going on, and when he was about the age at which curiosity begins getting the best of a boy his chance to find out finally came. His grandmother was invited to a dance, and she left (after warning him not to fiddle with anything). Naturally, he fiddled, and in the loft found, wrapped in animal skins, a dried-up owl's head made into a sort of headpiece. He put it on, and instantly became a screech-owl who flew out the loft-opening. He went from tree to tree, all at the will of something else, until he came to a house where someone was sick. He looked in the window, then went back home and took off the owl's head. He put everything back as it was and went to sleep.

The next night he followed his grandmother to a clearing deep in the forest. A group of people were burning a bundle of snakes above a fire; the blood and fluids dripped into a kettle. When he saw the gathering about to break up, he ran home ahead of them, terrified.

One day when he was older he asked her where she went on certain midnights. She quickly guessed that he knew more than he was telling, and looked at him with a new expression. "It's only for special people to know," she told him, "and only by joining the group can you learn." They went to the woods late one night.

His grandmother told the group that he had seen something of their mysteries, and wanted to become a part of them. The elders conferred for a while, then gave him his test: he had to drink the brew of the snakes, put on the owl cap, and fly to a house where someone they knew was sick. All he needed to do was point his finger at her, and return. His test would be done.

In the dimness it was not hard only to pretend to drink the brew from the wooden ladle. They gave him the owl's-head mask and he flew to the house of a sick young girl he had always liked. He saw her through the window and felt sorry for her, but he noticed a cat in her room, and, as a test, pointed his finger at it instead. It leaped up squalling and fell to the floor, dead.

The boy flew back to their meeting and told them he had done as they had asked, not mentioning that only a cat had died. By the next night, though, the elder witches had learned the truth. One of them came to the boy's grandmother and told her that he must die. The boy overheard this and ran to the chief of the nation, telling him the whole story.

The chief looked at him hard, as if measuring his courage in a glance, and then asked him if he would do something very brave. The boy agreed to go back to his home, to say nothing, and to guide the warriors of the nation that very night. As twilight drew his grandmother asked him with an eyebrow raised to go with her into the woods. He told her that he was not yet ready, that he had not had the heart to kill the girl, and that he had pointed at the cat instead. Seemingly fooled, she left alone.

The war party arrived and went with the boy into the woods, sneaking around the circled gathering. From time to time some of the witches told others to listen, saying that they heard noise; but the bravest of them only laughed. The leader of the witches called out something about the boy who had failed the test, who should be here; the grandmother rose to speak, but at that instant the warriors leaped (to the signal of a bird-call) and war-clubs struck. In no time each dim figure at the midnight commonwealth had fallen.

Because of his wits and courage and the great love he had shown for his people, the boy was adopted by the chief, and he went on to become a great leader. They say the witch who had first come to tell his grandmother of the boy's failure saw him talking to the chief and knew that the jig was probably up. This was the only one who escaped the destruction of the witches.

THE LITTLE PEOPLE

[In so many Iroquois supernatural tales the lead human characters ask the beings they encounter, "What sort of dance can I bring back?" It would seem that one of the most significant features of any individual mystical experience was the ritual it might impart to the nation. Many tales seem almost to serve as explanations (origin myths, in a way) for the cultural rites. One of the older Six Nations rituals is "The Dark Dance," and this, roughly, is its tale.]

One day a young boy out hunting came to the edge of a cliff in Zoar Valley and saw his target, a grey squirrel, in a high tree below him. He noticed two boys about his own age - supernaturally small - at the base of the same tree, shooting with tiny bows and arrows at a big black squirrel. Their shafts didn't even reach the creature's perch. The lad launched his own bolt; the tiny boys were astounded at the big mortal shaft that had brought their quarry down. The human lad approached, and was told that the black squirrel was the buffalo of the little people, their favorite prey. He was invited back to their village.

The father of the tiny boys told the Iroquois lad about the three tribes of the *Djogao*, the Little People. His own tribe were the Hunters (sometimes called "The People of the Underground Shadows"), ever on the lookout against the Great White Buffalo that roam the underground, and against all other evil monsters the Good Spirit put there for the safety of his Iroquois (who also call themselves "The Real People").

"The Stone-Throwers" are another group, folk of great power who often challenge the Iroquois to rock-throwing contests and other feats of strength. They seem to be water spirits to whom the Iroquois appeal in times of drought. They care for the natural balance in lakes and streams, freeing fish from traps and leading them to deep caves if the humans are taking too many of them.

"The Little People of the Fruits and Grains" make the plants grow and ripen. They are forces of nature, tutelary spooks who hide in the dark places beneath the forest floor, guide the young shoots into their flourish, tint the flowers, usher in the spring, and refresh the good plants. They fight blights and disease, and are the universal friends of the Native American people.

The human boy and his tiny hosts took a meal together. A thimble-sized bowl of corn soup, no matter how many times he drained it, never emptied. He tasted their berry juice and took a few puffs of the sacred pipe. Then the drumming and the dance began, and through the smoke the boy noticed many Little People. He was told to learn the dance well, for it could bring blessing to his nation.

He stayed what seemed like only a few days, and saw the rite enough times to remember it. When he returned to his village, he found he had been gone so long that they had given up hope of him. Yet the boy was a leader who soon had all his nation ready for the rite. True to his promise, the tiny old man came to sit beside him during the first Dark Dance, though only the boy could see him. Even today, the Dark Dance is held by the medicine society of the Six Nations.

Some Little People tales (like Irish fairy stories) have been recorded in the twentieth century. Author Leo Cooper (*Hayendohnees*) grew up on the Allegany Reservation, a member of the Heron Clan, President of the Seneca Nation, and a thirty-second degree Mason. From his childhood Cooper remembered two tales that appear in his book *Seneca Indian Stories*.

Cooper's little sister once believed two tiny children no one else could see asked her to come to the woods with them and play. Her mother took her quickly inside. Another tale involved one of his neighbors, a grown man hit on the head who would have died on the railroad tracks, but a flock of little people tugged him awake and saw him home.

ERINN MCELHANEY

THE VAMPIRE-HERMIT

There were rumors about the old man. He lived by himself far from the nearest village, but he did no harm; he was just apart, and odd. In his final sickness the villagers came to spend time with him and make his last days easier. Just before his death he said, "Put me in a bark coffin and set me in a corner of this house. Leave everything as it is, and hunters may shelter here when they are far from home. But no woman or child should ever sleep here," he said in a tone that should have been meaningful. "It will be just too dangerous." Strange as it sounded, all was done as he said.

Some time later a poor young man, his wife and their baby daughter were on a journey and came in this deserted house, thinking to stay there for the season. They saw the body of the old man in his birch-bark coffin in the back room, but made little of it. This was, after all, a normal custom for many Native Americans, whose acceptance of nature and all its processes was so complete that they often left their dead exposed to the elements, on scaffolds, or in shallow graves.

The husband was tired after returning from his hunt, and he lay down in the back room to rest. As his wife was preparing the evening meal with her daughter slung at her back, she had an uneasy feeling, and heard what seemed to be sounds of breaking bones, chewing, and slurping. She knew instantly that her husband had been killed, undoubtedly by some evil supernatural presence related to the corpse. There was no time for grief. Her thoughts now must be of survival... and for her child! Her only hope lay in deception.

"Your daughter and I are going to the stream to get water for the broth," she cried out as merrily as she could. "We're coming right back." She took the pail and left the house casually. When out of sight she started running along the well-worn footpaths toward the nearest village. She was a long way back toward it when a furious howl came from the direction of the cabin. The vampire had realized he'd been fooled, and his cry had reached her across the miles!

She ran even faster through the dimming woods, but her pursuer was coming. The next bestial vocable she heard was far closer to her than the first; the vampire-man was gaining. Trees behind her crackled! She threw off one of her scarves. In a little while she heard it ripped to tatters.

The noises neared again. She threw off another piece of clothing, and things were as before. Several more times this process happened, each time her escape was narrower; but she had run out of things to leave behind except her little daughter, and whoever wanted that was taking her first!

She was almost within hailing distance of the stockaded town, and set up a cry, the distress call of the Iroquois ("Goo-weh! Goo-weh!"), hoping someone might hear it. Some squaws were finishing their last chores outside the walls, and they took up the cry, not knowing what emergency was at hand. The running girl could hear their call being returned, and began to have the faint hope she might be saved! But the sounds behind her were terribly near. She could hear breath.

She collapsed beneath the trees outside the village, fearing it was too late. But a party of young warriors had burst from the village gates; she was within their torches' glow. She could not even talk to them at first, but they hovered over her, glaring outward into the night, crouching to defend her from all comers. This was the fighting Seneca, and even a vampire knew he was beat. "The luck was yours," called a half-human voice from the thicket. "We'll see what happens next."

We will indeed. The chief called women to care for the young mother, and set warriors to guard her through the night. The next day she told her tale, and a war-band set out for the hermit's cabin. They found the body of her husband, exactly as he had slept, but with a big hole in his side from the vampire's stealthy assault. Next to him in its coffin was the body of the hermit, on its face fresh blood and as contented an expression as a corpse can have.

The warriors howled their rage, and piled logs about the house. Soon a vengeful blaze toasted its contents, and they could hear yipping and howling from within. They guarded against all escapes, but despite their efforts, a big jack rabbit slipped out, dodged war-clubs, and dashed between the legs of a pair of warriors. This may have been the vampire-spirit and it may not; yet if it was, he had lost his human form, and evidently learned his lesson from the Seneca, because they never heard of evil done by him again.

TWO FRIENDS AND THE DEVIL
[This may be a morality fable about alcohol.]

In a Seneca town were two good friends, two very different young men. One was a quiet fellow who did the best he could; the other lived to raise hell. He drank; he stole; he lied; he chased married women; he even named his patron: *Hanisheono*, the Evil-Minded.

The good one tried to reason with him, urging him to do better. The bad one answered him fairly: "I've already chosen my god, but I'll never do anything to you. Our friendship will be strong until our paths divide." So it went, the good one trying to reform the other, the bad one trying to teach his friend the arts of the witch: shape-shifting into animal forms and making witch-light, poison, or love-charms.

The bad one got sick; the good one cared for him and tried to cheer him up. The bad one raved and thrashed; then, in a moment of clarity, he saw his god as he was, and addressed his friend: "Keep the grave-watch after my burial. The minute you leave me in those first three nights, the Evil-minded Spirit will dig me up and flay me, and use my form to do evil on the world. You can keep him from this."

Soon after dark the first night, the good man heard a sound like a chain dragged over the earth toward him and a voice beyond his small fire. It was indeed the Evil One, trying to persuade him to go home and be more comfortable, claiming that he had done enough work for a friend who had settled his own fate. But he stayed.

The next night it was the same story, but at the end of the third the good man weakened, maybe from fatigue, maybe because of the Evil One's bribe (a hatful of gold coins), or maybe because the Evil One was just too persuasive; he's known elsewhere for that. The good man nearly turned back when he heard a single awful scream. He stood on the moonlit trail, questioning the whole affair.

The next night in a dream his friend appeared to him, neither angry nor agonized, merely sad. "Wait till you hear about my god," he said. "The moment you left I was dug up and flayed; I died again. They also call him 'The Tormentor.' How he grins when he hears his name! I suffered, to say the least; but for the first time in his life the Evil One spoke straightly: to you, when he said it was all my doing.

"But know this: I will never do you any harm, even as the specter now I am. I will be with you all your days on earth, and you need never fear my image, if you ever see me again. Don't tell our people about the only time you failed me, because I wish to keep you from all blame. In life you were the truest friend any man ever had; in death, you will say the same of me. Now, farewell."

THE SWIG OF FLYING

[Seneca Cephas Hill (in Carl Carmer's *Listen for a Lonesome Drum*) gives us this sparkling story from the 1930's.]

Some young Seneca men only a year or two either side of twenty were hanging out one summer evening. The discussion turned to a group of ladies they were all dying to meet. The dullest of the group commented upon what a fine opportunity that evening's dance would have provided - at the Long House, ten miles away. None of them had access to cart or car, and by the time they could walk there it would all be over. The rest of them cursed their luck, and also the apple-head for not mentioning the dance when it would do them some good.

Hell may or may not have fury like a woman scorned, but we wager neither place holds anxiety like nineteen-year-olds in heat. The emotion probably moved one of them to do something he would not otherwise.

This was the host, a year or two older than the rest, about whom there were some unsettling rumors. No one knew what he did to get by, and some thought he "cut corners." This fellow went in his cabin and brought back a bottle. "Drink some of this," he said. Wondering what good it would do, they all took their swigs. The beverage tasted like sweet wine. The host replaced the bottle, and when he came back out, trotted off through the dark groves in the direction of the Long House. The others followed his lead, and soon all were running in great strides and bounds. They seemed to be moving effortlessly, but huge stretches of field, road and path went beneath them with each stride. They tossed back their heads and laughed to each other, dizzy with joy. The sky hurled above them.

In what must have been only a few minutes, their marvelous flight glided to a walk, and the lights and music of the Long House came to them through the trees. The trip itself had been so exhilarating that they had almost forgotten where it was heading, and at this point anything must have seemed believable. On their way in the owner of the magic wine cleared his throat and coughed. Red light glowed from his nostrils and mouth into his cupped fingers as if there were a flashlight or a fire inside of him. This was one of the traditional giveaways of an Iroquois witch, and a few old hands who knew that well would doubtless be within the Long House. "I wouldn't do that inside," said his best friend looking him in the eye, and the fellow nodded. They all had a good time and the effects of the flying liquor soon wore off, but the man who told the story to Cephas Hill stayed a long way away from that witch Seneca ever after.

SOME IROQUOIS BEASTIES

[Most of this lore is from the tales of DeWayne "Duce" Bowen, a Seneca storyteller who carries on the tradition of his ancestor, the legendary Cornplanter.]

The expansive, scenic Route 17 expressway links Jamestown, Salamanca, and Olean through the Allegany hills. Despite their beauty, these woods and vistas hold intrigue. How many of the admiring drivers sense the legends behind the trees?

Winter was the season for storytelling (according to talespinner and Seneca historian Duce Bowen). The Little People (in the forms of bird or bug) even had a compact to spy on mortal bards in the golden months and keep it that way. When all the Iroquois folk were in their longhouses, the traditional Six Nations storyteller arrived for a night of it with a bag. In front of his audience he spilled its contents: feathers, cloth, stones, sticks, anything. Before each tale the celebrated guest picked up an item, reminding him - so he said - of the story. Duce Bowen doesn't carry a bag, but he's given us many tales from the Allegany region. Here are a few.

WITCH'S WALK

The site near Salamanca through which the state routed its expressway "is considered to be a very haunted area," Bowen says. It goes along a trail once known as "Witch's Walk." One can only recall the old tales of the Iroquois witches, huffing along in the woody intervale on a frosty eve. No doubt any who were watching from beneath the branches, frozen in a stalking crouch, or perhaps silently waiting a meeting with an appointed love, held their peace and watched the more, at sight of the red lights, like inner fires, that came out the mouth and nostrils of the approaching walker. Only at night was it so easy to know them, as if indeed he or she had a fire inside, fanning itself the fuller as each breathed.

"Witch's Walk" - once it gave the railway a taste of its magic. The train used to go through this region, along the route of the current expressway beside river and hills. One night a conductor got off to check on something. He never got back on.

TALKING ANIMALS

There are stories about talking animals in many cultures. The Iroquois seem to believe we can catch them at it. Some of them are perhaps familiar horses and cattle, maybe even beloved dogs and cats about the home. Always their talk is in the native lingo, never any European tongue.

Whether this means that something else has disguised itself among your trusted animals, or whether your pet had hidden talents all along, we cannot be sure. But, according to Duce Bowen, "You don't want to walk by and see two horses talking to each other. You don't want to have an animal ask you why you're out and invite itself home with you." No we don't. Decline courteously, we would advise

THE GREAT SNAKE OF THE ALLEGANY

Supernatural portents precede human disasters in plays like *Hamlet*, *Julius Caesar*, and *Macbeth*. Awful omens were observed in the Aztec capital upon the landing of Cortez. Local events seemed to follow suit.

The 1960's construction of the Kinzua Dam had a terrible impact on the Senecas. Many lands dear to them (like the site of Cornplanter's grave) were lost, flooded by the waters of the new reservoir. A resurgence of new lore and revivals of the old seem to have greeted the situation.

Phantom horses along the roadways were some of the most striking modern apparitions (many seen by Whites), but one of the most unsettling was the Great Snake of the Allegany. Large snakes and related creatures are taken to be symbols of the earth. This appearance could represent one of many natural protests.

"Rolling Thunder Valley" is not far away, where the giant snake came out of the hills, down the valley and into the river. Since the Kinzua crisis more sightings of it have come, even by White sport fishermen. There are versions in which the men approach the bank of a lake or stream, barely noticing what seems to be a large log. At their first loud noise, it undulates off.

THE DEMON-BEAR

One of the fiercest creatures in the Iroquois supernatural zoo was the Demon-Bear. Very often this beastie is the alternate form of an evil wizard. There are those who look at all mythology as distorted recollection of real events. Could this be an actual memory? If so, we fear it.

In his dreaming Edgar Cayce raved that the Atlanteans shunned North America because its mammal predators were so nasty. This is one of the few times that archaeology even faintly supports Cayce; the late Ice Age's meat-eating megafauna were indeed dreadful, but the top predator isn't clear. It might have been a fearsome lion well bigger than our own African-style. The dire wolf was a rangy, swarming slack-jawed villain who would have liked his name. The saber-toothed tiger was another ghoul-faced fiend, a sickle-fanged bushwhacker. Yet a perennial top contender is the "short-faced bear," a formidable, long-legged goon that could run forty miles an hour. Was this the Demon-Bear? Any takers?

Zoologists have noted that big cats fear the bark of dogs; some conjecture this curiosity may be due an ancestral memory of a beast their forbears had to fear; was this the call of the short-faced bear? Animals may remember; couldn't we?

Allegedly, the Clovis point (an exquisitely-shaped flint spearhead) was the equalizer in early American man's struggle with the animals of the continent. If so, we admire them even more, dealing with such beasts with such a weapon.

HIGH HAT

The Six Nations have a legend that, after the mass extinction, the last of the Stone Giants fled to the hills of the Allegany region. There may or may not be some connection to the local bogie "High Hat," one of the more distinctive supernatural beings of the Seneca lands, and one of the more menacing.

High Hat is a swamp dweller, a cannibalistic giant never ranging far from his plashy haunts. He's a tall creature with a stove pipe chapeau and white gloves. From his descriptions, he looks like Uncle Sam, or the archetypal image of a White undertaker (tall, craggy, lank, and funky-hatted). We wonder how old he is.

Most troubling is High Hat's appetite for human flesh. The people who lived near his stomping grounds hung hunks of meat in the trees so he wouldn't dine on livestock or children. In one of Duce Bowen's modern tales, High Hat carries off a little girl and stows her up in a tree. This appears to be one of his tactics for keeping his game. (She's found and rescued before High Hat returns.)

High Hat, we would think, would be unique to the Western Door. Yet lore seeming to describe a similar spook comes to us from some marshy areas on the Texas-Arkansas border. The last local Native American sighting we hear of comes from the spring of 1970, though reportedly the White workers on the Kinzua site became so used to seeing High Hat from a distance, at dawn and sunset in profile at water's edge, that they even referred to him as "Abe Lincoln." "Anyone seen old 'Abe Lincoln' today?" was how it might go.

SPIRIT VOICES

The Iroquois seem to believe that at times, without a summoning, the spirits of the dead come back to the regions they knew in life. They may or may not return in image; but they are there, off in the distance of the woods and fields, manifesting almost as earthly phenomena, adding their natural carols to the music of the nights. On special eves, the visionaries among them (old women, most often, wise in the lore) can notice them, and even guide others to hear.

"As a child," recalls Duce Bowen, "it was a most impressive thing to sit down on those old porches. A grandmother would say, 'Be quiet, because so and so is singing.' And off in the dark you'd hear a person who had been dead for ten years."

We think on the consciousness of the urban citizen, the suburbanite, or the country-dweller, of almost anyone who has to deal with the urgency and detail of modern life. Figures, deadlines, bottom lines: how to turn them off? How hurried and cluttered our minds are! They sound within themselves, even with no other sounds around; they can drown out the outer tones. Which of us ever hears anything that takes long listening? Were it a country night and those choirs around us, chanting off in the trees of the approaching dusk - even the voices of our own beloved dead! - mixing among the dimming tones of the birds and the night-keener roar of the far-off roads... Which of us would ever hear them?

TRACK OF THE ILLUMINOIDS

One must speak sometimes in one way, sometimes in another, so that our real purpose should remain impenetrable to our inferiors.

Adam Weishaupt

THE SECRET SOCIETIES

As a general term, *illuminatus* (plural, *illuminati*) has always meant someone who has awakened in some sense - mystical, philosophical, or religious - from the largely unspeculative, materialistic tenor of everyday life. *Illuminated* can also describe someone exposed to the mysticism of the Western secret tradition (known as the "Hermetic-Cabalist" tradition, involving groups like the Templars, the Rosicrucians, and the inner circles of the Freemasons). Most specifically, the *Illuminati* ("The Enlightened Ones") were a secret anarchical society probably founded by young German law professor Adam Weishaupt in 1776. Like author Neal Wilgus, we use the term *Illuminoids* in the broadest sense, to refer to someone who fits into any of the above categories. This chapter concerns itself with the signs of such activity about the Western Door.

There's a vast literature and a whole mythology about the secret societies. Though this may seem more the domain of the conspiracy club, paranormal buffs are interested, too. It may look like a reach, but in the lore concerning them some secret societies are associated with magic, sacred magical objects (like the Holy Grail), UFOs, religious secrets, dark powers past mortal comprehension, and just about anything else potentially crazy mentioned in this book. Oh, and they have mystical philosophy at their roots.

One of the occult undercurrents concerns the deep interest the European secret societies had in the founding of the United States. To the unsatisfied of the Old World, the young nation in the New represented the last chance on the planet to begin again and create a perfect human society, perhaps as proof that humanity was in any sense perfectible. Mystical folklore attaches to the seminal events of the new Republic. Sacred architecture is widely evident about Washington, DC. Mystical symbols appear on our dollar bill. (The Great Seal of the United States has a handful of them.) Most of the founding fathers (Washington, Franklin, and likely Jefferson) were Masons, possibly Rosicrucians, possibly Iroquois-influenced mystics, and according to some "illuminated." Throw in John and John Quincy Adams (*maybe* members of a top-secret geomantic Druid outfit, the "Order of the Dragon," if there is such a thing) and you begin to sense the picture.

It's quite a tangle, all those theories about history, mysticism, conspiracy, and the secret societies. They lead everywhere, they never end, and it's hard to make any sense of them at all. We just don't get the feeling a world conspiracy is afoot, though it's fun to speculate. We hope this chapter can be fun. It's got some grim players.

BUFFALO'S MYSTICAL LAYOUT

[Our nation's capitol shared designs with the palace and gardens of Versailles, a sacred-geometrical layout if there ever was one. If Buffalo is like Washington in many particulars, our case is made.]

Washington, DC (said to be very haunted) was laid out according to late eighteenth-century mystical thought. Many of Washington's buildings and monuments, even recently-built ones, embody sacred architecture (a subject we discuss a little in our chapter on Roycroft) - most obviously the Washington Monument (modeled with Egyptian geometry after Egyptian obelisks). Streets converging on the Capitol and Lincoln Park were arranged to form solsticial alignments. (From the Capitol lawn on the Summer Solstice, the sun rises in line with Maryland Avenue.) Compass points (as in Masonic lodges and the Great Pyramid) were also critical quotients in Washington's layout. This makes little sense to most of us now, but it was a logical thing to do near the end of the eighteenth century, when, of course, this type of thought was not quite so offbeat.

The three great architects of the young nation were steeped in the philosophy of their day. An undertaking as important as the capitol city of the new, "perfect" nation would be worth doing right from the roots up. Landscape layouts would be part of the deal.

It was said that, in the design of our nation's capitol, four great intellects stand out: Washington, L'Enfant, Jefferson, and Ellicott. By the last name is meant Andrew Ellicott, brother of one of Buffalo's founders. The plot thickens from there.

The architect who gets public credit for Washington's design is Major Pierre L'Enfant, a French officer and engineer who had fought well in the Revolutionary War and was wounded at Savanna. He had risen from Lieutenant to Major of Engineers and was thirty-six as he worked on Washington. L'Enfant may have known his Masonic symbolism, but "his obstinacy threw every difficulty in the way," wrote George Washington (who canned him). Andrew Ellicott took over.

Andrew Ellicott by 1800 was the Geographer General of the US, a multifaceted man: a distinguished engineer who had already served on State boundary commissions, an astronomer, and vice-president of the American Philosophical Society (in the chair often occupied by Franklin and Jefferson).

If Andrew Ellicott was his family's occult philosopher, his brother Joseph was its mathematician. On his fortieth birthday (November 1, 1800) Joseph Ellicott became Resident Agent for the Holland Land Company, opening three million acres for settlement. His survey was based on astronomical observations and the establishment of meridians. Joseph may have assisted his brother Andrew at Washington, but it's sure they both worked on Buffalo. Their "wheel" plan for Buffalo (radiating streets) was based on the work of engineers at Versailles and Philadelphia.

The Ellicotts' 1804 street plan doesn't look too mystical to us, but we're going on what we're told. Of course, it's a much smaller setup than would be needed even twenty years later. Most of the streets have different names. (They seem tributes to rich Dutch investors and brother Joseph's Batavia bosses.) Even the street pointing straight to Niagara Falls is named "Schimmelpennick Avenue" and not its present Niagara Street. Yet it runs right through Niagara Square, which was obviously the nucleus of the young town. We suppose every city has to have a center; we wonder what made them pick that one.

Sometimes called "the father of Buffalo," Joseph Ellicott took a look at the mouth of Buffalo Creek and saw an ideal lake harbor he was determined to make into a city, "New Amsterdam." His mansion would have been in today's downtown, by the Ellicott Square Building and the old Iroquois Hotel, but the city fathers had other ideas. Old Joseph's inveterate talent for rubbing people wrong seems to have risen up and bit him, and the name and the site got away from him. Ellicott grew out of touch with Buffalo as the years went by, though he still considered the city his baby. Addled in later age, Ellicott infuriated clients of the Holland Land Company, and he was eventually fired. He committed suicide in 1826, some say in connection with the William Morgan affair. (He was a prominent Mason apparently into the matter up to his eyeballs.) Precisely what he was up to with Buffalo may have to wait a bit longer; but when one looks at the mystical connections at the city's very roots, it seems no wonder that some exceptional energy might still be at work.

THE SACRED LINES

[Your literal belief in the insights of this article may depend partly on your faith in "ley" lines (energy paths across the landscape) and the power of dowsing. Fair enough. The author keeps his mind open, as he advises others.]

In an attempt to learn what we could about Buffalo's mystic layout, we contacted an expert: Steve Nelson, a speaker and teacher well-known in esoteric circles. Currently living in Charlotte, NC, Steve is an astrologer, a geomancer, and a student of the sacred landscape. His wife Darley Adare - a consultant in the old Chinese art of landscape-magic known as Feng Shui (fung-shway, "wind and water") - is also a map-dowser. She can divine natural energy long-range. The enlightened pair set their sights on Buffalo, and took us in some directions we didn't expect.

It's quite reasonable to suspect that Buffalo didn't just "happen" into the shape it is. According to Steve's sources, Ben Franklin admired the Iroquois mystical traditions and believed in the power of the sacred landscape. He inspired the new citizens of the United States to shape their towns and villages along Native American patterns, which often followed natural energy lines in the earth. [When we pointed out to Steve that the central roadways of Buffalo and its region (Routes 5, 20, and 16) were all ancient Native American trails, he merely chuckled as if he should have guessed.] There was a considerable Native American mystical legacy in the region when Buffalo was forming. The Iroquois word *orenda* refers to the life-force involved with the sacred landscape.

Buffalo was settled decades before it was christened; yet the day of its incorporation (April 20, 1832) makes Buffalo, astrologically speaking, a first-degree Taurus city, with a grand trine (Sun, Moon, and Saturn) in earth. This is interesting, since the buffalo, the American animal for which the city is apparently named (there's some debate about this), corresponds to the European bull-symbol Taurus.

Buffalo's chart tells Steve that there are lots of resources in Buffalo, both spiritual and material. Its energies involve earth and water, the terrestrial two of the Greek four elements. This is right in keeping with Buffalo's stereotype as a blue-collar town: its citizenry will work hard and pay their taxes, but they won't set Hollywood on fire. Even today, in some circles the "New Age" landscape-mythology features Buffalo (with its northern bull-and-earth energies) as one of the four cardinal points of the nation. The others are Washington, Atlanta, and Los Angeles.

Buffalo astrologer Cassandra Joan Bauerle agrees with Steve that some inspiring changes may be coming for the region in the late 90's and beyond the year 2000. There will be breakthroughs in Buffalo, possibly in research and medicine. Many of Erie county's citizens should undergo great awakening. Buffalo will become more and more a place of pilgrimage for those seeking to "ground" their spiritual visions through its terrestrial forces. (We don't have to wait for the next millennium to confirm that; Buffalo's a good place to get "grounded" now. Whatever energy there is here tolerates only so much human pretension only so long.)

Niagara Square caught the eye of the spiritual couple, who felt sure this was the heart-center of the city. Through map-dowsing Darley identified three major leys (lines of force) at the core of the city, all radiating to (or from) Niagara Square. The big one comes down Niagara Street, pointing right to that power point Niagara Falls (one thing Steve and Darley couldn't have known from the maps we sent them). Another originates at Gates Circle (once an impressive natural fountain) and wends down Delaware Avenue. The third is Genesee Street, which (as Buffalo geomancer Franklin LaVoie observes) heads right to an earth mound. Is it ancient and man-made?

Steve notes that these leys are the spiritual lifelines of the city, beacons of power that lure all kinds of tappers, natural and supernatural. He points out that most of the haunted sites in his native Charlotte are along leys. Steve's feeling is that somebody (possibly Joseph Ellicott) dowsed the location of Niagara Square.

Though the Square is not precisely an octagon, the streets that once shot from it in eight directions evoke that symbol to the same effect. Furthermore, the classic Feng-Shui pattern known as the *bagua* fits quite neatly over the shape of the Square. Its location and composition - its obelisk, fountain, and siting - make it, geomantically speaking, a rare accumulator of telluric power. The Square brings energies in from all the leys; it's a "resonator" for the entire region. "When they're at the center of a convergence of streets," reports Steve, "obelisks are like tuning forks. The 'vibes' go in all directions."

Though New York is a Leo state, Steve senses that Buffalo is an earthy spot of it in need of an energizing influence, like fire. He suggests that a big garnet (the state stone, a fire-symbol) placed at Niagara Square would start giving the region a better balance of Leo energy. A perpetual flame might help here, too, where an ounce of prevention would be pounds of cure. It's perhaps in keeping with Steve's recipe for Buffalo that lions - symbols of primal fire - were placed here about the McKinley Monument. (Even they seem to need a zap, though; they're lounging leos.)

We may have gotten a look at these forces in the 1970's when the mid-city beautification project of Mayor Stanley Makowski's administration brought the public to a curious outrage. "Improvements" to Niagara Square turned it into a brickwork bagel only muggers and revolutionaries would have appreciated. Behind its terra-cotta crennels the square's graceful lions barely peeped, its Classical fountain cowered, and its pale obelisk shot startlingly skyward like a missile ready to launch above sandbags. It perhaps affirms the spiritual significance of the site that simply obstructing its view touched such a nerve in the circling motorists one would have thought too busy to notice. Long into the rising rhetoric, the Mayor backed his planners. With several hundred thousand taxpayer dollars, "Fort Makowski" was eventually dispersed, and in many minds the phrase came to stand for a good man's embattled term as mayor.

Map of the
VILLAGE of NEW AMSTERDAM
(now the City of Buffalo)
Made for the Holland Land Company
by
JOSEPH ELLICOTT, Surveyor
1804

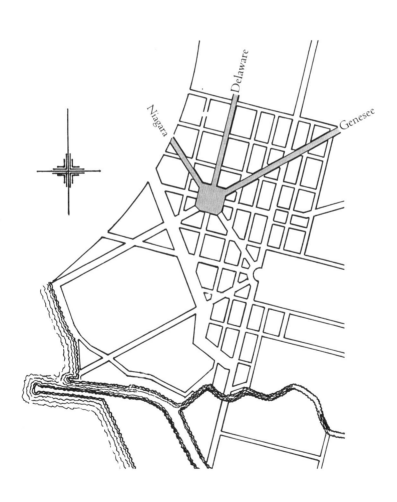

THE MOHAWK MASON

[His name shot terror through the northern colonies in the second half of the eighteenth century - Joseph Brant (*Thayendanegea*) - "The Devil of the Mohawks." One of the most infamous episodes of the Revolutionary War was this engagement in the Western Door, and it involved an original Mohawk Mason.]

By the middle of the eighteenth century, the Iroquois had overhunted their homelands and were ranging far afield in search of game. On such an expedition in northern Ohio Chief Joseph Brant (1743-1807) was born. Forever remembered as the archetypal Mohawk, he was a member of the lowly Wolf clan, probably descended of Huron captives. Educated by his British patrons, Brant fought for them at Forts Ticonderoga and Niagara, and in several campaigns of the French and Indian War.

He stood against a tree in a frozen instant at his first war-encounter, the fifteen-year-old Brant at Ticonderoga. The gun-cracks, cannon-thunder, tomahawk-blows, the saber-clash, the cries... Smoke, and his feathered comrades circled among the trees. He stood amazed, sensing his life shifting like a seesaw; but he recovered in the breath (else his term as a war-chief of the Iroquois would never have begun), and he whooped into the fray like the rest. His valor and competence made him a chief; ten years later he sailed to meet the English king. (Below decks and in irons on that 1776 voyage were Ethan Allen and some of his "Green Mountain Boys," taken prisoner at Montreal by Crown forces including Brant.)

Brant and fellow ambassador John Hill *Oteronyente* quickly became celebrities in England. London's Tower was their favorite monument, and its Swan with Two Necks their favorite Inn. The young Mohawk and King George III were quite impressed with one another. "A finer man," Brant maintained "it (would) be a truly difficult task to find." The King thought Brant such a famous fellow that he sponsored his initiation into the Falcon Lodge of the London Freemasons. Upon his return to the land of his birth, there was work for Brant again: the colonies were in open rebellion.

Though Joseph Brant will always be associated with the massacre of Cherry Valley (which took place in traditional Mohawk territory near the Hudson River), he spent much of his life about the Western Door. The other outrage linked to him occurred just west of Conesus Lake, not far south of Rochester.

George Washington and his top advisors had decided that the key to their northeastern defense lay in taking the Iroquois out of the war. Stinging guerrilla assaults and infamous massacres had hampered military action and rocked American morale. General John Sullivan's 1779 campaign aimed to break Britain's Iroquois allies and stiffen withering Yankee spirits with revenge.

Sullivan's was a formidable expedition for the day, several thousand forest-fighters, well armed and trained. For the most part, it was disastrously successful. It routed 1,500 Tories and Native Americans in a battle near Elmira, and the underbelly of the Seneca territory lay before it. It seldom caught its subtle foes, but it burned villages and vast stores of crops. This latter aspect of the deal proved the most tragic, for it killed thousands of noncombatants through starvation. One detachment of Sullivan's army met a portion of the tragedy it dealt.

"The Boyd-Parker Mission" - twenty-six men under the command of young Lieutenant Thomas Boyd - were out looking for a major Seneca town when they were caught in a ravine by Tories and Senecas. Fifteen died in the first fusillade; a handful tore their way out with knife, tomahawk, and clubbed musket. Only Boyd and Parker were taken alive. At Cuylerville neither would reveal the Yankee battle plans. It's an old, persistent story that Boyd - a Mason like Brant - flashed a Masonic "help" sign (a hand signal) to the Mohawk chief, who responded with one of his own; then the two young officers were given to the "Torture Tree" (whose descendant still stands on the spot), with no mediation from the Mohawk Mason.

The Masonic affiliation of an Iroquois chief was not really much of a surprise. The Masons welcomed prominent people of all origins. It was perhaps more startling that anyone expected "The Craft" to mend the wartime conduct of a Mohawk chief.

To some Brant's apparent refusal of the Masonic help sign meant there was no check on his bloody lust. To others, it reflected the mid-1700's split between British Masonry and the other forms, Continental and American. The combatants in the American Revolution certainly arrayed themselves along those lines. Some even regard the Revolution as a war between Masonic affiliations. In that sense, Brant may have been an illuminated agent.

Joseph Brant, though a stern warrior, was surely not the "savage" some thought him. He built the second Protestant church on the Niagara Frontier in Lewiston around 1760. Some say he was not present during the massacre of Cherry Valley, and that he wept at his first look at the carnage. Others believe that the episode of the fabled "Torture Tree" also took place when Brant was away from the British-Iroquois camp. If so, blame falls on the White Tory father-son team of Walter and John Butler, at least for failing to prevent the torture by their Iroquois charges. It was once said, though, that the Butlers could "out-savage the savages." No dreaders of the devil their actions declared them, the Butlers might not have feared to act in the place of Joseph Brant.

Though the Mohawk - Britain's solidest Iroquois friends during the Revolution - had earned no gratitude from the young United States, their treatment was some better than eighteenth-century minds might have expected. Brant was a man of ability who went on to peacetime renown. It may be unfair to link him with two great wartime crimes. He did kill his own grown son in a knife-fight in later years, so maybe the old war-temper could not be underestimated at any measure; yet it may always be a mistake to pass modern judgments upon people of earlier times. We tribute Joseph Brant as a man whose spirit burned brightly all his time on earth.

THE GENERAL'S BARRED WINDOWS
[Arch Merrill (*Shadows on the Wall*) pointed out to us this suggestive tale.]

"Bloody Corners" it once was known, this small Allegany County town. The hill and valley people used to duke it out at the crossroads, but when its citizens sought to improve its fortunes, "Friendship" seemed a more inviting name. At the intersection of Main and East Water streets is an ample, charming white house, once with forbidding bars on its lower windows. The man who put them there was George W. Robinson, one of three Mormon exiles who came back east.

Edward Wingate and Sidney Rigdon were his fellows, defeated dropouts from the schisms that marked the early years of the Mormon faith. Like Robinson, big "Ned" Wingate had married one of the Rigdon daughters. Wingate had also been a high-ranking officer in the Danites, the Mormon "secret police."

When Rigdon joined his daughter in Friendship he was a beaten man, having lost his struggle in the Mormon church to the able Brigham Young (without whom, it has been said, the Mormon faith would not now be with us). Rigdon had been one of Joseph Smith's confidants and second in command. Some say that he (not Smith) had written the Book of Mormon. Till his death in 1876, Rigdon denied this stoutly, and anything else that might have hurt the Mormon faith.

These three refugees came to Friendship to live out their lives away from the halls of prophecy and power. Though some (eager, perhaps, to discredit Mormon) reported that they recanted their faith, disinterested observers refuted it. There was some other reason for them to live in fear; some intrigue must have surrounded the matter.

Robinson (one of the town's foremost citizens) established a store, a mill, and a bank. The villagers called him "General" (possibly because of his imposing manner, possibly due to his former Mormon rank), and his house was one of the finest in town. One day two men came to Friendship looking for the Mormons' onetime treasurer. Robinson grabbed a satchel, took the train (reportedly to Buffalo), and came back to Friendship only after they were gone. Then the bars on the windows appeared. No one could imagine what jewel or secret he held that could not even be trusted to his own bank.

Rumors concern hidden treasure, explosive secrets, Mormon mysteries, and maybe even some possession of the Prophet himself. We have no speculation beyond that. Today the bars are gone, and condominiums made of the fabled house. Do its tenants sense an aura of the secrets it may have held?

WILLIAM MORGAN AND THE ANTIMASONIC FURY

[If we have any image of the Freemasons at all, many of us probably envision middle-class World War Two vets in funny hats who march in holiday parades, call themselves "Shriners," and help children and charities. Not all suspect that the Masonic past is swathed in mystery and occultism. One of the worst blows ever dealt the public image of "The Craft" landed right here in Western New York.

The attempt to make sense of William Morgan's disappearance plunges one into a flurry of warring conjecture, revealing just how much his case was on the minds of his contemporaries. We do our best to summarize the many opinions, and intend no disparagement of the modern Masons, guilty, as far as we can tell, of nothing but good work.]

"Somebody told me to drive like hell," testified the driver of the coach, "for there was a man inside who was bound for that place." One of the most famous trials of mid-nineteenth-century America was underway, and a scandal that would distract the nation for decades.

The outlines of the story are not in dispute. Batavian William Morgan (sometimes styled "a quarrelsome drunk") was struggling to support his wife and child, and hit upon the idea of writing a book, an expose of the Freemasons. It's not certain that he even was a Mason, but someone took the matter very seriously. On September 11, 1826, William Morgan was accused of stealing a shirt by the master of a Canandaigua Masonic lodge. The charge was dismissed upon the spot, but he was arrested again almost immediately over a debt due a tavern owner (another Mason) and thrown into a Canandaigua jail.

The next night, several Masons arrived and took Morgan away. His most likely last stop was Fort Niagara, where there was a fiery conference over his fate. The point of all the sound and fury was to get Morgan to turn over the manuscript of the book he and Batavia printer David C. Miller were readying to publish. Evidently, Morgan refused. He was never heard from after.

A nationwide furor led to lengthy public trials during which several Masons were jailed and the two major political parties scourged each other. Though it was impossible to find and convict the presumed killers of Morgan, even to learn for sure his eventual fate, by no means did interest in the matter cease.

In the spring of 1828 in Leroy, NY, the first convention of Anti-Masons was held, establishing a credo that Freemasonry and free government could not coexist. They set up a committee to keep the matter public and establish a state convention at Utica the following August. They organized to promote candidates in county elections, and the first third party ("The Antimasonic Party") was a major player. Though by 1838 it merged with the Whig party, several times it had come within a few thousand votes of electing the New York State governor. Famous politicians (including DeWitt Clinton and Millard Fillmore) cut their teeth as anti-Masons.

Why was the public so quick to rile against "the Craft"? First off, there was the strong suspicion that the Masons were under oaths that transcended any form of religious or national allegiance. There was resentment against any who would be the judges, jurors, and executioners of an American citizen who had broken no laws. Antimasonic sentiments may have become energized by the class war often lurking beneath the surface in American politics. The events of 1826 were not the beginning of the matter.

At the crack of the nineteenth century, prominent clergymen in England, France and New England had come out hard against the Illuminati, Adam Weishaupt's legendary, probably defunct political group (founded Mayday 1776) that, for a time, infiltrated Masonry. The international uproar of 1799 made it all the easier to panic three decades later when Morgan disappeared. Who were the "Illuminati"?

Except for some vestiges of mysticism - largely used as their own secret code - the Illuminati sound like early Marxists with a penchant for Classical code names. Plotters "Gracchus" Babeuf and "Anarcharsis" Clootz joined promising convert "Lucian" (a proverbial scorner of religions), and the modest Weishaupt himself ("Spartacus," heroic freer of slaves). It seems a real stretch of reason to think they could put across even a quick plot, much less a historic one. Two Illuminati agents sent to help the French Revolution were promptly guillotined. Some were so delighted to be involved in something secret that they couldn't resist blabbing. In 1785 an Illuminatus named Lanz was struck dead by lightning and his satchel of sensitive documents published. Under the single order of a German duke, droves of Illuminati turned themselves in, piously swearing off the Illuminism business. They sound like the gang that couldn't shoot straight.

But what about Morgan's book, *Illuminations of Freemasonry*, published soon after its author vanished? "A more absolutely inconsequential mess of rubbish was never printed and bound," stated E. W. Vanderhoof sourly, summing up the consensus. Morgan and Miller seem like blackguards all the way, betraying their oaths for money and doing a dull job of it besides. Masonic exposes had been around for over a century, and Morgan's book revealed nothing new. None of its passwords, grips, nods or motions could mask an outsider in any Masonic lodge more than half an hour. There was outwardly nothing in the book to get its author killed - which makes us wonder if it represents what Morgan really knew, and what secrets the Masons had left in 1826 that they would kill to defend.

Underlying all the teaching and practice of "the Craft" is "the Masonic Secret," a profound, utterly unspeakable truth which proper initiates can discover for themselves after much trial and study. Most Masons probably never arrive at this revelation, and there may indeed be nothing but speculation behind it; but was that what Morgan had? More prosaically, some suspect that Morgan may have been about to expose not mystical secrets, but corruption in the local Masons. Some of those involved in his disappearance were later implicated in "cooking the books" at the high offices their Masonic affiliation helped them attain.

William Morgan's disappearance will probably never be explained. Most think he was killed and pitched weighted into the Niagara River, though a number of other theories have been proposed. Letters came from various parts of the world for decades, purporting to reveal that Morgan was living secretly and well.

The affair had curious fallout. Mormon founder Joseph Smith (always fascinated by Masonic ritual and regalia) took Morgan's wife Lucinda as one of his many, and we wonder at her involvement in matters. She identified a body which, it was later proven, could not have been Morgan's.

By now this famous murder-disappearance has firmly entered the folklore of the Western Door. The Ridge Road across its northern stretch (upon which Morgan was allegedly transported) sports a psychic coach and Morgan's ghost at several stops along the way. Carl Carmer (*Listen for a Lonesome Drum*) mentions the families who live along the old Ridge Road and their legends of the Morgan mess. "They say that sometimes even yet beneath the apple-blossoms in the orchard a lamb is born with a thin red line about the white fleece of his throat - as all lambs were born in the spring that followed the fearful murder over a hundred years ago. And they say that after a hot September day of toil they sometimes wake to hear the beat of hoofs (muffled by dust though now the road is paved), and that if they dare to look out they may see by the moonlight a carriage, curtained, black, drawn by a steady trotting team, rolling westward through the night."

Morgan's monument still towers above a Batavia cemetery, erected by the Masons themselves (probably gritting their teeth), less a tribute to the contentious boozer than a hope of repairing their own image. It would be decades more before the spotlight shifted and hid them once again in open sight.

THE ROSICRUCIAN RASCAL

[P.B. Randolph's Western Door connection may not seem very direct, but if the reader of this book can grant its writer some indulgence - only here do we directly ask it - we include him in our study. Randolph - adventurer, mystic, author, lover, feminist, and undoubted illuminatus - is one of our favorite characters.]

One of the most charismatic people of the last century was a mixed-blood mystic named Paschal Beverly Randolph (1825-1875). Also the biographer of the Buffalo Brothers Davenport, Randolph was born in New York City of Native American, African, and European ancestry. Abandoned as a child, he went to sea and, by the age of twenty-eight, was exotically handsome, had worked at a number of trades, developed an interest in Spiritualism, and toured upstate New York as a self-educated physician and preacher. His first ventures at recognition were letters detailing messages he had received from the beyond, sent to the *Spiritual Telegraph*, a New York City Spiritualist magazine.

By 1854 the spirits persuaded Randolph that the time had come to speak as well as write, and in Auburn, NY (already famous for its psychics per square mile) he addressed the Harmonial Convention of "the Poughkeepsie Seer" Andrew Jackson Davis. So inspired at the podium did Randolph become that the spirit who spoke through him before lunch took up without missing a beat after it.

In 1856 Randolph spent plenty of time around Buffalo writing his biography of the Davenports. "Johnny King" still manifested through the two teens, but the book about them waited until 1869.

The young mystic's aspirations called for larger pastures, and he moved to New York, calling frequently at the offices of the *Spiritual Telegraph* to deliver, it would appear, impromptu auditions by way of spirit-speaking. We can only imagine the effect of these freelance seances on callers and magazine staff alike, however devoutly Spiritualist. The launching-stages of a mystic seem no more dignified than those of a rock star. Yet Randolph may have developed psychic gifts; he played a mean game of chess while blindfolded, and like another psychic of a later day - Edgar Cayce - was in demand as a healer, prescribing cures while under trance.

Randolph attended the London convention of the disciples of Robert Owen to read a message the American spirits had sent through John Murray Spear (of Harmonia). Because of the number of more famous speakers, he never made it to the stage. To Randolph this symbolized yet another racial and social cut, but it worked to his advantage; he was made by his next move, a Paris seance before Napoleon III.

Randolph became a popular professional psychic, touring North America and Europe. In Egypt, rites involving hashish made a deep impression on him. The drug was incorporated in his philosophy and formed the prime ingredient in his "elixirs." He did substantial mail-order trade in these concoctions. Another Oriental feature that impressed Randolph was the use of sex in ritual magic. He was ever the pioneer, and many women found him enchanting.

Like many Spiritualists, Randolph was an ardent social reformer, an opponent of slavery and an exponent of women's rights. He went to work for the Union cause during the Civil War, recruiting Blacks for the effort and using his oratory to good effect. After the war, under the direct suggestion of "Honest Abe" Lincoln (whose Spiritualist inclinations are widely suspected), Randolph moved to new Orleans to teach the emancipated slaves.

By the late 1860's Randolph was disillusioned with politics and even racial prejudice in his own Republican Party. In Boston he set up the "Rosicrucian Rooms," sort of an early New Age head shop: trinkets sold and readings given. He also ran into legal trouble, involving, as one might imagine, any number of his own cutting-edge activities. The matter ended tamely.

In the early 1870's Randolph's misfortunes came to a head. Not only was he swindled of most of his earnings, but he was crippled in a fall from a raised train track in Toledo, Ohio. Nevertheless, he made another trip to Europe, founded another secret society (initiating Peter Davidson, who went on to found the "Hermetic Brotherhood of Luxor"), and married a nineteen-year-old. (Their son Osiris Budh Randolph became a successful and legitimate MD.) Always moody and often drunk, Randolph shot himself to death in Toledo in July 1875. (At this moment on another continent, Theosophist founder Helen Blavatsky had a vision in which the magic bullet Randolph shot against her went into himself.)

Randolph was a prolific author, writing books of pure fiction as well as philosophy. He still appears in many anthologies of Black writers and influenced a number of Rosicrucian-inspired groups. Because of his use of drugs and sex in magic Randolph came to be known as the model for the wilder Aleister Crowley (born the year of Randolph's death). Had we heard of him in the 1970's, Randolph would have been a hero to the author and his fellow underclassmen. Randolph stands out now as a metaphysical soldier-of-fortune whom we only could have wished, alas, a happier life.

THE GRAVE OF JACK THE RIPPER

[They've been dying to hang this one on a Yank for a long time, and it looks like they've finally done it. New light has shined on the Ripper case, and it shadows a Rochester gravestone. We thank a neat bit of work done by two English policemen: *Jack the Ripper: First American Serial Killer*.]

In three Autumn months of 1888, an unknown fiend killed and mutilated five women beneath the Whitechapel section gaslights of Victoria's London. The public was outraged; herculean efforts were made to find the killer. British wit gave "Jack the Ripper" his memorable name, but it has always been stymied giving us his real one.

The utter absence of any firm leads fed the wildest speculation. Conspiracies - even black magic - were thought at work, and "Ripperology" soon became a hobby. At least a hundred and thirty suspects (almost all of them disqualified out of hand) - from Queen Victoria's grandson to Impressionist painter Walter Sickert, from loopy Lascar sailors to cracked kosher butchers - have had their advocates. The murders were so explosive and demonic that it was hard to believe their perpetrator had never struck before; it had to be a visitor to England. The blade-work seemed to bespeak a knowledge of surgery; the "foreign doctor" theory settled in and stayed.

No profile was as popular as the "mad American." (The English must presume madmen so common here that one would only stand out if he travelled.) One famous suspect was Scottish-born doctor Thomas Neill Cream (1850-1892), who grew up in Canada and studied at McGill. At least four women died at his hands in America, and during his London stay the same pattern broke out. This time the Metropolitan Police got their man. In the noose at Newgate Prison, Cream raised a mighty cry to ring him into whatever nether Valhalla waits human fiends: "I am Jack the.... Gack!" Some think he was trying to say, "Ripper." If so, "the equally-evil twin" theory is needed; the Whitechapel murders took place as Dr. Cream was in an Illinois prison.

Another prominent candidate buried with a long neck was Pole Severin Klosowski (1865-1903), better known as "George Chapman." A violent womanizer and a surgeon's apprentice, Chapman lived a year in New York City (where killings suspiciously like the London ones started). He matched the only likely description of the Ripper (a man seen with one of the victims just before her murder). The full depth of his evil may never be known; but Chapman was a poisoner. Watching his trusting victims slowly fade before him seemed the point of the thing.

In 1993 several old letters connected with the Ripper case came before Paul Gainey and Stewart Evans, two Suffolk, UK, policemen. One of them (from Chief Inspector John Littlechild, head of Scotland Yard's special branch during the Ripper murders) had been in an attic for forty years after its 1913 composing, and with a bookseller since. Littlechild's letter to a journalist revealed that those closest to the case in 1888 had had a *very* short list of suspects, and presented one that had somehow slipped through all the cracks.

American "Doctor" Francis Tumblety was Littlechild's prime suspect, an occasional visitor to England where he hoped to set up a practice. Blood on his shirt after the last Whitechapel murder made his landlady turn him in. Inspector Littlechild thought they had their man, but bail was granted. Tumblety fled to Paris, then wound his roundabout way back to the States. Ripper-style murders happened in Jamaica and Nicaragua, possibly on this homeward saunter.

Born around 1833 in Canada, Francis Tumblety grew up "a weed" on the banks of the Rochester canal. The youngest of eleven children, Irish-American Tumblety was a neglected, emotionless child. He surfaces in adulthood as an herbal healer and full-time citizen of between-the-lines-life. Used to aliases, he was ready to bolt at the drop of a name. He made money, but trouble always seemed near. At 32 he was arrested and questioned in the assassination of Abraham Lincoln. No stranger to the London police, Tumblety tried to involve himself in the Irish struggles and under an alias may have bought the knives used in the famous 1882 assassination at Phoenix Park; but he was too flaky even for terrorists. He was 55 at the time of the Whitechapel murders.

How a man in public life could hide from Scotland Yard is curious, but not a mystery. The sexual offenses to which Tumblety could be linked were not extraditable in those days, and once there was some ocean between the parties, the Yard could only watch. Tumblety never made his fatal move. How he hid from Ripperology is another story, and partly explicable at official behest: if Scotland Yard couldn't catch him, it was not eager to proclaim that it had let him go.

Ironically, many who profiled the unknown Ripper but never thought of Tumblety caught him pretty well: a woman-hater, vain, antisocial, unassertive, with deep needs for notoriety. In its obituary the *New York Herald* mentioned Tumblety's arrest in connection with the London murders which, curiously, had coincided with his visit.

Jack the Ripper may seem an unlikely illuminoid, but there may be a link. Letters signed "the Ripper" came to Scotland Yard, but the only likely sign from the fiend himself was a bizarre verse chalked on a wall above a bloody apron in the early hours after a murder:

The Juwes are
The men That
Will not
be Blamed
for nothing

Tumblety too wrote queer poetry, had they only known; but, fearing a riot, the top investigator had the message erased. The deranged ditty looked illiterately anti-Semitic, and it seemed possible that a Ripper-happy mob might invade London's Jewish section. (The suspect-of-the-week was

John Pizer, a Jew soon cleared.) A cooler head transcribed the message, but we could have had a photograph - which waited only full daylight - in the hand of the Ripper.

As spelled, the term Juwes (pronounced "joo-ees") figures in the lore of Masonry. The brothers Jubelo, Jubela, and Jubelum (nicknamed "the Juwes") are the primal Judases of the Craft; they killed the first Grandmaster (Solomon's architect Hiram Abiff) who would not betray the Masonic Secret. (The marking of the poor prostitutes seem similar to one of the proverbial Masonic punishments for violating oath. The apron beneath the verse on the wall might symbolize the Masonic "lambskin.") In one theory, the murders were done to hide a secret, perhaps a sexual one, known only to the prostitutes of a certain prominent Masonic "John," maybe even a member of the royal family. The Ripper may have been an Illuminated agent, and the murders either warnings or sacrifices.

The ditty gloats that the "Juwes" are not "blamed for nothing." This seems to affirm that the three brothers were blamed properly: that they actually committed the murder, or that there *was* something to steal. The verse may affirm the existence of "the Masonic secret." This is no indictment of the modern Masons; no other murderer taints his or her entire group, and knowledge about the Masons was widely available from many sources. But whoever the Ripper was, he seems to have had Masonic symbolism on his mind.

As a final indignity on top of posterity's suspicions, Tumblety's name is misspelled ("Tumuelty") on his stone at Holy Sepulcher Cemetery. Ironically, a century after the Ripper's London heyday, Rochester knew the same visitation. Eleven women were murdered and mutilated by Arthur Shawcross in the late 1980's and 1990.

In the Ripper's wake, the social conditions that led to a desperate class - upon whose substance-dependent women the Ripper preyed - were on everyone's conscience. They still exist to some extent, and we call for compassionate, unending efforts to find real remedies. If the Ripper did any good, it was in drawing Victorian England to see itself. Still, if there is a hell, may he and those like him howl within it.

THE SUPERNATURAL ROYCROFT

LAURA WILDER

Nenikika se Solomon
("Solomon, I have outdone you.")

Emperor Justinian, 537 AD

EAST AURORA'S MYSTICAL COMMUNITY

In March 1994 the author gave his first public talk about the mystical roots of East Aurora's Roycroft community. "The Supernatural Roycroft" (in the former Roycroft Chapel) was well attended, and during its course the speaker stood behind his evidence. He was not sure everyone would like it.

Perhaps sensing some new assault upon East Aurora's foremost citizen - Roycroft founder Elbert Hubbard (1856-1915) - many aficionados and townsfolk had long been cool to the idea of Roycroft occultism. During their exposure to it, the listeners' reaction could well have been outrage, but they were keeping it to themselves. Yet at the end, the late Rixford Jennings - a widely revered figure who had been an original Roycroft artist - rose from his seat and toddled up to the lectern. He was a small, ninetiesh man who now walked very slowly. People seemed to wait for him to speak. We braced for what could have been a blast from this oak of the Roycroft community.

"You know, I remember Elbert Hubbard," Jennings said. "Some of his friends used to hang around at the house when I was a kid. I always knew there was something weird about those guys." His eyes twinkled above his white mustache and mutton-chops. "You know that (artist) Sadakichi Hartmann? He was *really* weird." The august little gentleman mosied off. The author felt he had arrived.

It's always surprising how famous someone can be in life and how forgotten two generations after. Elbert Green Hubbard - an early feminist and a pre-Woodstock longhair - was one of the most influential men of his day, but his name is hardly a household word now. A rich soap sales-man by thirty, Hubbard retired to become a speaker, an author, a journalist, a publisher, a country philosopher, and the founder of East Aurora's Roycroft community. He was an advertising pioneer who did not shy away from political debates, and this is probably what doomed his posthumous notoriety. Hubbard - the philosopher of entrepreneurship - trod on the toes of a few too many of those who would go on to become the arbiters of posterity's taste. It could also be that he excelled in no single field; Hubbard was a Jack of many trades.

Founded first as a fine printing operation in 1895 East Aurora, Roycroft soon became an Arts and Crafts Movement community that produced generally high-quality products in many media, selling them through the mail worldwide. Hubbard and the small campus of Roycroft buildings at the center of the town soon became world-famous. Through his writing and publishing, Hubbard put across to America and the world an entire Roycroft philosophy of "head, heart, and hand": thought, love, and work. We think there's another level of Roycroft understanding.

We have three basic observations about Roycroft:

 Sacred architecture is demonstrated at the Inn and other campus buildings.

 Founder Elbert Hubbard had mystical interests.

 There is a tradition of paranormal folklore at Roycroft, particularly the Inn.

Roycroft does not seem one of the active paranormal sites in Western New York, but it may be the most mystical one when all factors are considered. Though in recent decades many popular books have brought sacred architecture and geomantic ("earth-magic") traditions into prominence, a century ago sacred architecture in a non-religious building was a sign of something, probably that its builders had exposure to occultism. We take it as such at Roycroft. We think Hubbard sprinkled signs of his own mystical interest throughout his Roycroft endeavors, and that he attracted people of like interests to his enterprise.

While the subject of Roycroft occultism raised no eyebrows among Hubbard's contemporaries - it was hardly remarkable in the Arts and Crafts Movement - to almost every reader now the theme will need development. That's the purpose of this chapter. We'll toss in a few of our favorite Roycroft ghost stories, too.

There is still some supernatural gossip from time to time about the Roycroft Inn and Campus, but it's not often of the convincing kind. Don't expect to visit Roycroft and see a ghost. Do, however, expect to get a good feeling. Write, sketch, meditate, shop, stay for dinner, stay the night, or just walk around. A lot of the old feel is pretty fragmented by the changes over the years, but you can still find little nooks and corners that have it. Never forget, though, that the little town at the heart of Western New York has at its heart an old and unsettled mystery whose roots may go back to other lands and the oldest human knowledge.

SACRED ARCHITECTURE
AT ROYCROFT

"Sacred architecture" is a style of building that, in a broad sense, expresses certain shapes and attitudes reminiscent of religious shrines, presenting the beholder more or less an aura of sanctity - a "churchy" feel. In this sense, many turn-of-the-century architects (like Frank Lloyd Wright, E. B. Green, Louis Sullivan, and, as we hope to demonstrate, Elbert Hubbard) qualify, and the average person might notice their effectiveness.

In a more rigorous definition, sacred architecture expresses ancient mystical philosophy through its shapes, ratios, siting, and alignment. It's found virtually everywhere in the world. While in most cultures sacred architecture has always been pretty mainstream - simply a style of building reserved for temples or other structures of cultural significance - in the West it's been underground for the last few centuries. Most recent people who built with sacred architecture were exposed to the mysticism of the secret societies or others (like the Shakers and Mormons) who preserved old traditions.

We notice something else about sites built with sacred architecture: they tend to collect a lot of ghost stories. Whether it's some force liberated by the shape, siting, or alignment that affects human consciousness (causing people to see things), or some other effect, no one can say. Experiments at sacred sites - particularly megalithic ones - have discovered geomagnetic irregularities.

Some architects in Elbert Hubbard's lifetime employed sacred architecture, possibly as a stylistic feature like a poet's decision to use rhyme or meter. Indeed, the Arts and Crafts Movement was a revival of old traditions in all the arts, among which was architecture. Sacred architecture might have had its first popular revival in *The Seven Lamps of Architecture*, the first book of Classicist and art theorist John Ruskin, a major influence upon Hubbard.

So far as we know, Hubbard himself was the virtual architect of his own "beloved pile." The accounts we have show him strutting around the site in progress, demonstrating roughly what he wanted roughly where. There is suspicion that Hubbard may have taken some counsel from local architects (even a Seneca mystic), but the picture illustrates one more page in the book of this impressive self-made man. Frank Lloyd Wright was said to have been unimpressed with Roycroft's design (particularly the Peristyle, resembling works of his own). That's saying no more, however, than that Shakespeare might have found shortcomings in Hubbard's literature, or Plato in his rumination.

Critical parts of many famous and not-so-famous religious structures worldwide are located over underground peculiarities - blind springs (probably Stonehenge), caves (Teotihuacan's Temple of the Sun), gas wells (the temple of the Oracle at Delphi, and Lackawanna's Basilica), and faults. Roycroft, as far as the dowsers can tell us, is located over a source of underground energy, probably a strong blind spring or crossing streams. This is discussed more fully in the article on the Ruskin Room.

Markus Kessler, a Buffalo architect familiar with the Inn, pointed out in 1992 that the subtler ratios of sacred architecture are discoverable only after trained and tedious measuring, none of which has been done for Roycroft. (We doubt it would turn up much when we consider the damn-the-torpedoes manner in which the Inn was raised.) Yet in the broad sense, the Inn and many Roycroft buildings certainly qualify as sacred architecture. Several features confirm that at least the gesture has been made.

Several trapezoidal arches about the Inn Kessler finds "Egyptianate," or suggestive of the turn-of-the-century mystical fascination with all things Egyptian. Yet when one comes to a look at the inner structure of the south wing - the hotel - of the Roycroft Inn (as almost no one ever does), a very curious thing develops.

The basic shape upholding this three-story wing involves several (likely three) trapezoidal arches of mammoth wooden beams behind the rooms, stairs, and Salon. This formation was only obvious during the restoration when some walls were stripped away. It's architecturally sound, but quite unusual, resembling in two dimensions the shape of the flat-topped pyramid found in Mesoamerica, in the Middle East, in Southeast Asia (such as Angkor Wat), and in the roof of Hubbard's own Ruskin Room. Steven Groh, another Buffalo architect, reacted with a sense of certainty that it was a form of deference to Egyptian influences common among the "new-wave" A & C artists of Hubbard's day (and among mystical outfits for centuries). Hubbard showed mysticism even in hidden ways.

When explaining his own motives, Hubbard seems to have delighted in ambiguity. He let on that he styled the Inn after Wordsworth's church in Grasmere, England. Wordsworth's Church looks little like the Inn. There may be invisible correspondences between the two; no one knows of them yet.

THE ROSICRUCIAN CONNECTION

[The Roycroft community had a general leaning toward metaphysics. Theosophists and Christian Scientists were among its members, and perhaps other devotions were represented as well. Elbert Hubbard's expressions of mystical interest are broad and ambiguous. We think he sought the light in a number of directions, but his most direct link is probably to the Rosicrucians.]

On October 4, 1984, at a gathering in the Roycroft Inn, Elbert Hubbard was given the Humanitarian Award of the San Jose AMORC ("The Ancient and Mystical Order of the Rosy Cross"). This honor was about seven decades posthumous.

The *Rosicrucian Digest* of 1985 asserts that Hubbard had been part of the council that elected Spencer Lewis Imperator of the AMORC (probably in 1914). It also claims that Rosicrucian symbols are embedded in the foundation of the Inn, and that there are affinities in Roycroft writing and architecture to the spiritual and metaphysical traditions of the Rosicrucians... and the Iroquois.

The Rosicrucians are outwardly Christian, and their interest (like that of most mystical societies) is in human spiritual development. Their sources seem to be the traditional ones of other European groups, chiefly that pipeline of mysticism called the Hermetic-Cabalist tradition. Their themes tend to be antimaterialist: spiritual purity, progress, and ascension. Among their traditional images are the rose and the cross, even though these may not be the source of their name. (That, it has been suggested, is two Latin words meaning "the dewy cross," not the rosy one.)

The Rosicrucians claim many of the famous departed, who protest little through ordinary channels; yet this one may have claimed the affiliation himself. Rosicrucian themes and imagery appear in Roycroft art. (Elsewhere we discuss the first Philistine poster.) The squared rose most famously drawn by Dard Hunter has become symbolic of both artist and community, and, as it appears, evokes the "squared-circle" of so much old mystical thought. (Squaring the circle meant unifying opposites, both of male and female nature and of earthly and spiritual planes. Some think the pyramid is an attempt to enact this idea in architecture.)

The Roycroft name itself is suggestive. Its two syllables evoke the initials (R and C) so commonly used to signify Rosicrucian artists or themes. Hubbard gave several explanations for the name of this enterprise; it came either from "the Roycroft brothers" (English craftsmen), or from French terms meaning "King's Craft." Maybe so, but "King's Hill" and "King's Tract" would be more direct meanings of the name. In the undercurrents of mystical literature, "King's Hill" would imply some sense of geomantic significance to a site, perhaps implying that it was laden with power. "King's Tract" (property) is even more suggestive. The phrase *Rex Mundi* ("King of the World") keeps coming up in mystical lingo. Its meaning is debated.

As Frances Yates has shown in *The Rosicrucian Enlightenment*, there is probably no ancient group of philosophers at the root of the fabled Rosicrucians, and the modern orders who claim the title have no line of descent from the ancient wisdom. Several early-seventeenth century pamphlets about the mystical Rosicrucian order may have inspired like-minded people of the day to form their own societies behind the same heavy name. Yet since the late Renaissance, there has been great interest in the idea of these mystic, benevolent philosophers, and, in Hubbard's day, resurgent interest in the group itself.

A band of European painters - the *Salon de la Rose + Croix* - embodied Rosicrucian imagery in their works. The Scottish group called "The Glasgow Four" (known to Hubbard) were decidedly mystical in all directions, including Rosicrucian ones.

The Rosicrucians have certainly established an occult pedigree since their first manifestos. Their connections with the traditional Masons, as well as the recent Theosophists, possibly the sinister Illuminists, and maybe even the old Templars, are widely rumored. In the nineteenth century a number of Rosicrucian-inspired groups took off in many directions, not all of them savory. (If there is anything anyone wanted covered up in the Hubbard file we suspect it's this, the "guilt by association" of his secret societies connection. Those eager to preserve Hubbard's reputation might worry that a public not versed in the fine points would associate one form of mysticism - Hubbard's quite certainly benign kind -with all, including the unsavories.)

Almost too obvious a clue is Hubbard's adoption of the nickname "Fra," short for *Frater* (Latin, "brother"), traditional term of address in some monastic orders. It also addressed one of the Knights of St. John of Jerusalem, later the Knights of Malta, the only warring-monk order to make its way to the present in anything like its former form. Maltese-like crosses appear here and there in Roycroft art and design. Though not famous for it like the Templars, the Knights of St. John too were associated with occultism. "Fra" is also an alteration of a common form of address among Rosicrucians.

Most western mystical groups - like most of their members - have ties to others. We see no reason to deny that Hubbard was interested in mysticism, and that he alluded to this interest between the lines of his Roycroft enterprise.

THE

RUDYARD KIPLING
FRANCIS WILSON
PHILIP BECKER GOETZ
STEPHEN CRANE
ELBERT HUBBARD
WILLIAM McINTOSH
H.P. TABER
EUGENE R. WHITE
GELETT BURGESS

PHILISTINE

THE FIRST PHIL POSTER

[Though author Timothy Neat says little direct about Roycroft, *Part Seen, Part Imagined* (about the Scottish artists called "The Glasgow Four") led us to many of the insights expressed in this article.]

In 1891 a group of painters dedicated to Rosicrucian themes put on an exhibition in Brussels, a historical center of European Rosicrucianism. The *Salon de la Rose + Croix* included Josephin Peladan, Carlos Schwabe, and Jan Toorop. Their display - a key step in Symbolist painting - caused a storm in the art world. It was advertised by Schwabe's poster, a famous example of Rosicrucian symbolism.

The interrelatedness of opposite qualities is at the heart of Rosicrucian thought. Adherents see life as a quest, a journey from darkness toward a greater light, from earthly materialism toward knowledge and spiritual immortality. The idea of such a journey is the basis of the symbolism of Schwabe's poster.

Mysticism does not exactly dominate Roycroft art, but there are signs of such an interest. One of the most persuasive is the poster advertising the December 1895 first edition of the *Philistine*, Elbert Hubbard's career-long quarterly magazine of literature and comment.

The term "Philistine" has long meant someone lacking artistic taste; it seems an odd choice of title for a magazine. In Hubbard's estimate, the historic Philistines were a Biblical tribe with a reputation as cultural goons who may have simply opposed the trends of their day and come out on the short end of a historic propaganda campaign. To Hubbard, conformity to any establishment - even the artistic one - was a sin; hence, in Hubbard's paradox, it was backhanded praise when certain parties (doubtless including his own critics) called one a Philistine, a reflexive insult triggered by questioning trends common sense could not defend. Hubbard could hardly have denied, though, that the term carries other baggage. The Bible accuses the Philistines of worshiping Beelzebub ("Lord of the Flies") and of stealing the Ark.

The first "Phil" poster is a convincing sign of occult interest, showing Rosicrucian themes of rebirth and spiritual ascension. The winged, shrouded back of a haloed, male figure - unmistakably Hubbard-like (because longhaired) - gazes from a Classical veranda into sunrise or dusk. The figure's forehead is framed by a bright disc, possibly from close range. The wings about this halo make the solar disc (a well-known Egyptian-Rosicrucian image). Hubbard's head within it forms the "dotted sun" - an image from the Egyptian hieroglyphics newly popularized and beginning to appear throughout other mystical art of the late 1800's (like that of "Glasgow Four" mainstay Charles Rennie Mackintosh, artist, architect, and likely Hubbard acquaintance).

This poster (whose elements it seems likely Hubbard was prescribing) is essentially a Theosophical, and probably Rosicrucian, painting. It was commissioned by Hubbard - or so word goes - of an artist named Dwight Ripley Collin, about whom no information seems available to the *American Book of Poster Art* (which speculates that this name may be an alias). Whatever the D stands for, there are those R-C initials again, suggesting either "Roycroft" or "Rosicrucian." [The R-C initials have often been used to cover the identity of Rosicrucian artists. In a literary magazine of Hubbard's day, for instance, the name "Rene de Coutans" was widely presumed to stand for an anonymous Rosy Cross writer, author of a mystical poem.]

The possibly lunar disc pearling the forehead of the backward-facing figure ("illuminating" his brow) is very suggestive, possibly saying in coded form that Hubbard was "illuminated." (See "Track of the Illuminoids.") It may be something related to it that Hubbard acquaintance and sacred architect Frank Lloyd Wright named one of his homes Taliessin, after the Welsh poet whose name means "Shiny Brow." Stairs have often been symbols of spiritual progress; the fact that the Hubbard-figure has reached the top may imply that Hubbard himself was "ascended."

This poster has troubling implications. For one, the Egyptian "dotted sun" glyph - the circle around a spot - was used by the Illuminati to refer to themselves in their documents. It could be read to imply Hubbard's membership in that anarchic group (which we doubt). One might also note that each evidently made-up name of the poster's artist contains six letters. 666 is the number of the beast, the traditional Antichrist, and ultimately Satan. (Hubbard was called that and worse in his lifetime, never fear.) This also is not as it appears.

Entertainments like the film *The Omen* have popularized some symbols associated with satanism (like the number 666), to which not all of them properly belong. The matter would not be complicated if the early Christians had had a short list of enemies. Among those on it were the Gnostics, a Judean group whose philosophy (Christian-like, but evidently not enough) has been very influential upon a host of Western mystical groups. Indeed, many of the historic secret societies were formed as underground religious groups, though they may have lost that prime function before long. Some of the things popularly associated with Satan (like 666) also have Gnostic significance. It's hard to be sure of the interpretation of such symbols in relation to Roycroft, except that satanism never enters the picture.

THE SON OF SHAKESPEARE

The unforgettable Elbert Hubbard was responsible for a number of forgettable novels, page after page of discursive journalistic philosophy, and a lengthy series of imaginative biographies (the *Little Journeys*, probably the best statement of his literary achievement). An incorrigible quipster, all over his magazines Hubbard made references to places, things, and people that we are hard put to follow. These allusions included occult subjects and terms.

One of the most direct literary expressions of Hubbard's occult interest appears in his first published novel *The Man* (1893), co-written, many suggest, with his confidante and second wife Alice. (The author's name was given then as "Aspasia Hobbs"; the real Aspasia was the mistress of another man not short on self-esteem, the great Athenian "Golden Age" statesman Pericles.)

This odd book (in need of an editor) tells the tale of "a man" living near Buffalo who forms a platonic relationship with a liberated (for the day), spiritual young woman. As their philosophical friendship progresses, it develops that the man is hundreds of years old, and, as a matter of fact, the son of Shakespeare whom no one thought survived. [That coat of arms Shakespeare had them award his father (to make himself an instant nobleman!) went to waste.] His Italian mother - doubtless the "dark Lady" of the sonnets - had taught Shakespeare the arts of the Italian stage. It may be worth pointing out that Rosicrucian associations are rumored of Shakespeare, and even stronger ones of Francis Bacon (whom some take to be the real Bard).

Whatever he says about himself, this then-300-year-old wise man is obviously a mystical adept. The proverbial Rosicrucian master (as well as many similar magi throughout literature) also has a supernatural life span. At the end of *The Man* is a rehash of the old alchemical motif: the mob attacking the lab.

It's a natural tendency to interpret a book in terms of its author's life. If the characters in *The Man* are anything like those in East Aurora, the lady-confessor was Hubbard's younger, deeply spiritual paramour. Hubbard himself would have been the vastly wise, supernaturally powerful mystic.

One of the most curious features of *The Man* is what happened to it within a few years. Of course the book was not the success its author envisioned - few are - and Hubbard triumphed in other venues. Then he tried, apparently, to quash the book. Hubbard bought up all the copies he could and got rid of them. A few scattered originals survive, and it's doubtful if the Library of Congress could be persuaded to part with its copy.

This says to us that Hubbard might have been ashamed of the book. [Knowing this author's reaction to his own juvenilia (which the world in its callous mercy could not be persuaded to publish), it is the same thing he would have attempted if those dreadful saps of mortality had ever seen the light of publication.] Yet we are also well in mind of the conspiracy club, who might see this as one more sign that Hubbard eventually attained what he sought so fully that he had no need to seek his mystical "big break" publicly any more, perhaps even attempting to cover up all trace that he ever had. [Francis Bacon and Descartes made overtures (more straightly than Hubbard's in *The Man*) to the Rosicrucians in their day. The idea of a secret group of philosophers seemed captivating to famous lonely philosophers.] In that light, Hubbard's subsequent mystical allusions seem almost like smirking lead-ons.

Some Masonic authors in a different context make a big deal out of the sheer phrase "The Man," as if it were a heavy occult password, but for now enough is enough. *The Man* says to us little more than that Elbert Hubbard thought of a story and wrote it. It says also that mysticism and magic were not far from his mind, and that at that point he saw no reason not to display this interest directly.

THE ROYCROFT CHAPEL

KENNETH SHERIDAN

THE ROYCROFT SEAL

[Many familiar symbols and images - like the rose, the lion, gold, and the pyramid - give clear impressions to the average person; they also have deeper meanings, and this may be part of the process in their use by parties who do not wish to be direct about anything, even the fact of their concealment. There is considerable ambiguity to the Roycroft seal.]

One issue should be dispensed immediately. The Roycroft seal - the double-barred cross atop the circle - looks like the Nabisco mark (upon which we won't speculate, though occult rumors often swirl about heads of state or industry). There was even a lawsuit over the matter, ending with the award of a dollar (which we think Hubbard paid), and the agreement that Roycroft would not bake crackers if the National Biscuit Company would rein in its urges toward art. That said, it should be added that, like Blanche Dubois, the Roycroft seal has long relied upon the kindness of strangers; it's had a life of extensive use.

Hubbard claimed the mark came from a book printed in Venice in 1472, that it was used as far back as 1300, and that he was ignorant of its meaning. "If I ever find out I'll change it," was his summary of the matter. He may have known more than that.

The seal seems to go back about as far as it could. Colonel Howard Vyse found this mark twice in Campbell's Chamber of the Great Pyramid; it was thought a mason's stamp meaning "A-Okay." A mark like the seal appeared in Renaissance painting and medieval allegory. Attempts to track the the orb-and-cross shape itself turn up mystical overtones that point back to the ancient Near East, that hotbed of religions. This image is found on coins, medals, inscriptions, even the throne of the dark god Baal. Names like Babylon, Persepolis, and Phoenicia keep coming up in the quest for this image. "Regeneration through water," antiquarian Sabine Baring-Gould thought it meant: "Life eternal."

In three days of 1896, *Buffalo News* editor William McIntosh went from urging Hubbard (unsuccessfully) to make a company of his *Philistine* magazine (which McIntosh would partner) to blasting its religious views and use of a sign (evidently the seal) of Dagon, fish-god of the ancient Philistines. Roycrofter Marcus Quinn called this seal "a Dagonic device" whose meaning he was not inclined to set forth.

The Roycroft mark has a haunting quality, as if we should recognize it from somewhere. It's almost a generic symbol, an amalgam of others familiar to the mystical Arts & Crafts movement:

The Tree of Life. From the Hebrew cabala, this is one of the most seminal images in the west. Usually a lengthened-diamond pattern of ten spheres, it has many styles; some (like Charles Rennie Mackintosh's version) are indeed like the Roycroft seal.

Dr. John Dee's *Monas Hieroglyphica*. Renaissance mage and Queen Elizabeth's astrologer, Dee came up with a seal of his own and a book about its mystic meaning. Dee's *monas* is biomorphic (even seductive) next to the rugbeater Roycroft seal, but similar - a circle with lines.

A blend of alchemical symbols. According to 20th-Century writer "Fra Albertus" (Hub's virtual pen-name), Roycroft's seal looks like two old ciphers merged: inverted signs for saltpeter and orichalchum, or brass. Alchemy even gives us the stylized "R" (*radices* - roots) to go inside the orb. This formula would hardly make gold, but if anyone knows what the devil it might be about, let them write the author.

A blend of Medieval symbols. The top of Roycroft's seal is the "patriarchal" (double-barred) Cross of Lorraine (an old French crusader family). The bottom - the orb with partitions - is a Medieval symbol representing the world. As it stands the meaning of this glyph might be "Lorraine rules the world!" - not so wild when you hear the occult baggage the *Holy Blood, Holy Grail* club gives this family (related to "Rosicrucian King" Frederick of the Rhine, who surfaces again in our look at Roycroft).

An alteration of the Egyptian ankh (a teardrop-topped tau linked with life and regeneration). Roycroft's seal looks even more like something called a "nefer," another Egyptian symbol of wholeness.

A mason's mark. Several sacred geometrical systems were used by Medieval masons. Each group had its trademark of circles and slashes which, when tested, the mason had to explain or "prove" off of one of the several "mother diagrams" representing the group's philosophy.

One of the Rosicrucian seals in the AMORC handbook is (with a triangle replacing the orb) identical to the Roycroft mark. The Theosophical Society was also fond of cloning new symbols from old, many of which have been incorporated into their seal. Roycroft's has the aura of some of the watermarks studied by Lionel and Patricia Fanthorp in their book on the French Rennes-le-Chateau mystery.

We have no faith in any explanation of the Roycroft mark. It's entirely possible that direct evidence - Hubbard's own direct words - will surface from a letter or some such source to clarify the matter. There is, as always, one possibility left: that any deeper associations of the Roycroft mark are entirely coincidental, and that Hubbard's surface comments, varied as they are, represent his thinking about it. It sure does walk like a duck, though.

MAGNA MATER

[We could have discussed a number of Hubbard's mystical friends, but that only makes the case with association. We chose one he and his wife chose: the sculptor of an odd stone.]

Katharine Emma Maltwood (1878-1961) - antiquarian, artist, author, mystic - is remembered for her discovery of "The Glastonbury Zodiac," patterns on the Somerset landscape that seemed to be the classic figures of astrology. She sought spirituality through deep delving into the traditional old wisdom of Europe. "The Hubbards chose Katharine Maltwood," writes Rosemary Alicia Brown, "(to provide) the visual inspiration of a work embodying their ideals."

Formerly part of a fountain in the grotto (now the parking lot to the south of the Roycroft Inn) *Magna Mater* ("Great Mother," on page 155) is a high-relief sculpture in Portland Stone. Its critics were generally pleased with a piece they found Egyptianate and (like so many other things Roycroft) archaic. *Magna Mater* brought Alice Hubbard to tears.

A roughly square figure like a Stonehenge-arch (with Egyptian-Classical influences) makes a cave about *Magna Mater*, a huddled crone who broods above arms on knees. From a space at her right tiny images of infants pour down; up into that at her left heads a whirl of adult figures. A dramatic inscription ("Great travail is created for every man...") is beneath the earth-mother's shackled ankles. To look at this and other Maltwood sculptures is to view inspirational, basically classical images cramped into crabby spaces, seemingly bursting from the stone - an Ayn Rand novel condensed into a page.

By the 1920's Maltwood seemed hooked on Madame Blavatsky's theosophy, sensing the wisdom of the ages in the zodiac. Maltwood describes her chill of awe, gazing out on the Somerset landscape and scrying this circle of giants. Aerial photographs indeed dimly suggest them, formed by streams, rivers, hills, canals, ancient earthworks, roads and paths - but only an artist would have spotted them, and only a mystic would envision them. Maltwood immersed herself in the cycle of Arthurian tales, suspecting that the Holy Grail was less an object than a lost secret perhaps still recoverable through arcane study. Europe's oldest mysteries - like those at the secret levels of Templar, Masonic, and Rosicrucian orders - were keys in the search.

Magna Mater now sits in the garden of the Elbert Hubbard Museum in East Aurora. After nine decades of weathering, its Portland Stone looks a lot like concrete. Its cascading babies could be a pile of grapes, and only in old pictures is its motto clear; yet its creator was a worthy Roycrofter.

THE RUSKIN ROOM

"The great Victorian" John Ruskin (1819-1900) was an art and architecture critic who was enormously influential upon Elbert Hubbard and the entire Arts and Crafts Movement. Ruskin advocated a return to medieval style and craftsmanship in the products of everyday life as a way of improving its quality. Though his image is not that of an occultist, Ruskin had esoteric interests. In his twenties he wrote the book that made him famous, *The Seven Lamps of Architecture* (on Gothic architecture). He was also a trustee of the British Society for Psychical Research.

The room named for him at Roycroft is the spot most immediately suggestive of sacred architecture. Atop the squat tower at the northeast corner of the Inn, its pyramidal roof outlines the generic mystical symbol recycled in Pythagorean geometry and societies such as the Masons and Rosicrucians. This pyramid is flat-topped like the great one in Egypt. [There is even a famous Roycroft cartoon in which Hubbard is portrayed as the Egyptian pharaoh Rameses (with three pyramids clearly visible in the background).] A cupola with windows to the four quarters - essentially an observatory - originally capped the Ruskin Room, suggesting the astronomical function of classic sacred sites and "The Eye in the Pyramid" on the dollar bill. (This structure was taken down early in the twentieth century.)

The Ruskin Room, like all else at Roycroft, did at least double-duty, but it was rumored to be Hubbard's study and the site of Rosicrucian ceremonies. Modern gossip gives us a handful of oddities in this room: light and sound effects, seances, magic rites, clairvoyant experiences, poltergeists, and apparitions (even images of Hubbard).

Sprouting from each of the sides (minus one, the western) is a sort of gable, a separate peak with its own window. This gives the roof of the Ruskin Room seven corners, which may or may not refer to the seven-sided tomb of Rosicrucian founder Christian Rosencreuz.

According to an old town fable, a Seneca shaman showed Hubbard precisely where to site his Ruskin Room. Several dowsers ("water witches") unaware of each other found energy beneath the Ruskin Room (like what is found at key spots of some famous ancient religious monuments).

If there is some source of earthly energy about certain spots in major preindustrial religious sites (or postindustrial mystical ones), it may be this that accounts for the paranormal reports. Many researchers are beginning to think that this force has some effect on human perceptions. Maybe it can make people see things that are not really there; maybe it increases the odds people will see what really is.

THE FACE ON THE CHAPEL

[An architectural feature for which our late friend Austin Fox (*Church Tales of the Niagara Frontier*) had no explanation is surely worth a closer look.]

In a high gable on the north side of the Roycroft Chapel is a red, bas-relief, bearded face. It's right there on Main Street in open view, but few ever notice. It was apparently put there at the building's construction in 1899 by Roycroft sculptor and blacksmith Jerome Connor, known to work in terra cotta. It looks a bit like the *Wizard of Oz'* cowardly lion, and Oz illustrator W. W. Denslow was indeed a prime Roycrofter. We know of nothing else like it at Roycroft.

Some say this face is the North wind (not commonly thought of as red). In most drawings, the winds appear open-mouthed and with familiar gusty breath. This one looks far more like old images of the lion, a prime symbol in Renaissance alchemy and astrology. It surely seems to be the focus of the gaze of Michelangelo's statue on the Middle School lawn across Main Street.

The bearded, paternal face resembles traditional depictions of sky gods, and reminds us of the Mormon "sunstone" of their Nauvoo temple. Twin pairs of rays from the cheeks and beard suggest pyramidal angles with the ground. (We think again of the pyramid-roofed Ruskin Room.) The pyramid evokes - like the lion - the esoteric symbol of primal Fire, the kingly element.

The face on the Chapel reminds us of William Blake's painting "The Ancient of Days." This shows the mighty bearded Creator reclining on the clouds and reaching his hand down from the firmament. Beams from his spanned thumb and forefinger (similar to those from the cheeks of the Roycroft face) make the old Masonic symbol of the compass. This painting, like much of Blake's work, seems to show the influence of Gnostic ideas. Blake's figure is looking down into the world, and the Chapel-face looks more out across it, but the attitudes of the two are similar.

So far no one has explained the face on the Chapel, but we like to think (on the basis of no evidence whatsoever) it may be linked to a Renaissance German monarch, Frederick of the Rhine, the Elector Palatine, the so-called "Winter King," and sometimes styled "The Rosicrucian King." Frederick established a short-lived court in which all forms of philosophy thrived, and to which alchemists and magicians flocked. He became a hero to the secret societies ever after. Frederick's coat of arms contained a man-like red lion, and in the political cartoons of the day he was portrayed by that image. We have yet to hear any other explanation for the Chapel-face, so we'll play with that one for awhile.

SOME ROYCROFT GABBYJACK

[We do not know if all of these stories are "true" in the literal sense. We do know, how-ever, that they were truly told: the tellers believed. "Gabbyjack" is a Hubbardism for gossip.]

HAG OF THE GIFT SHOP

At grey twilight once in the late eighties, just before Christmas, the author walked up the short pathway to the Roycroft Shop and stumbled into a developing curiosity. Two clerks - a longhaired male artist and a young woman - were conferring in excited tones, holding up and peering into a framed painting. They told their tale.

An old woman had come in a few moments before. She had stalked around, looking at what was on the walls, even peeping into the corners as if to interrogate them, muttering to herself as if indignantly addled. Finally she marched to the desk and demanded to see Elbert Hubbard. Her manner presumed that he was in hiding somewhere about the Campus, not seventy years into the Irish Sea, and that those employed at Roycroft really knew where he was. It was almost as if she had stepped into the century's ninth decade from out of its second with none of the years intervening, and suspected that the old rascal still orchestrated every aspect of the place as he had before.

The clerks could only stammer their confusion. At last, the old woman scornfully turned to go, slamming the door behind her. It was a miracle that the glass didn't break; but the loud sound that followed was that of the painting, flying from its perch on the heavy fieldstone wall - opposite the door and twenty feet away - and landing face down on the hard floor. It was a reproduction of the first Philistine poster (with its metaphysical connotations). This the two clerks were examining, staring from it to the door and back again.

THE LEGENDARY HALLOWEEN

The old festivals, which seem to land at such seminal times about the year, can provide opportunities for heightened spiritual experience. One of the most talked-about paranormal events in the lore of the modern Roycroft involves a Halloween eve back in 1984. The night - which has become proverbial - commenced in the Ruskin Room (then more or less a bedroom-museum) with some waitresses and bar people holding a seance. A number of them occasionally experimented with psychic communication in the late 70's and early 80's, seeming to regard it as another amplification of a recreational drug experience. The seance took the form of a test of "psychometry," in which people with closed eyes tried to get impressions about objects placed in their reach by the others. Things uncomfortably broke up when one woman (who since became known as a psychic) came unglued over a framed picture. It was a photograph of Elbert Hubbard taken right before his first step onto the Lusitania. Weeping uncontrollably, the sensitive was overwhelmed with oppressive images of cold, darkness, water, and suffering. The seance - which had started in the tone of a party game - was uncomfortably over.

Someone then - it was about eight o'clock - noticed that the paintings in a little room they called "Alice's Office" (just behind the bar) had all been turned askew. The same person had arranged them properly just hours before. (Though years later one employee smirked that he had caused the alleged paranormal effects in this room, we doubt he can have accounted for the whole rumor cycle.)

The night's greatest drama was yet to come. The natural festivities in "Ali Baba's" basement bar were marred by a host of supernatural ones (including spontaneously shattering shot-glasses and stereos turning themselves on and off). Even bizarre human behavior seemed to accompany the matter, which culminated in an ugly brawl.

THE RETURN OF ELBERT HUBBARD

One of the more colorful legends of the town involves the reappearance of Elbert Hubbard - his ghost, his apparition, his revenant, his evil twin, whatever. There are many versions of this tale.

An eccentric gentleman used to claim that in the early seventies he had regular conferences with the venerable founder of Roycroft through the old photograph then mounted behind the bar, on its north wall. This was a large green-tinted picture of the front of the Inn at the early part of the twentieth century. The Master of Roycroft used to walk down the steps of the Inn in this image and confer with the drinking gentleman as he sat at the bar. The effect must have been like conversing with a television.

Another local legend has it that "The Fra" used to walk the streets of the town on windy, gloomy nights. With a different gentleman he was reputed to meet and confer about matters of life and afterlife. The teller of the tale claimed to have received great guidance in this fashion.

Another common legend involves the appearance of Hubbard-like apparitions about the Inn. In the Ruskin Room he is bowed above a book in study by a Dard Hunter stained glass lamp. Of course, when someone charges up the winding stairs there is no one in the room, and the lights have been turned suddenly off. Sometimes there are hints of occupation immediately preceding - a still-rocking chair, the click of the lights turning off, maybe the lamp's dangling switch-chain.

THE ROYCROFT DEMON

Several people point to encounters with a terrifying presence at the Roycroft Inn, usually associated with the cellars. One tale involves a former Inn handyman and another worker who were so overwhelmed one night back in the early 70's that they rushed from the place in a panic. The other (who described some horrifying "thing") never came back. The handyman, though, - who had experienced only a feeling - had a faith bordering on reverence in the essential goodness of Hubbard and the old Roycroft. So does the author, but he doubts he would have done like the handyman, who took his sleeping bag back down there and spent the night.

Other such tales involve sudden, gloomy, overpowering feelings, so vivid that they produce instant panic. A hard-minded manager fell victim to the meltdown malaise. Never any sort of believer in the Roycroft's magic, one night he returned upstairs from an after-hours foray to the mens' room in "Ali Baba's" bar, knees knocking and pants still around his knees. Something had come over him so overwhelming and sudden that he hadn't even buckled his belt before starting to run. The storyteller still chuckled thinking of his silky powder-blue undies.

A SECOND GIFT SHOP TALE

The Roycroft Shop is one of the loveliest little buildings in Western New York. It's an art gallery, a storehouse of charming, quaint and upscale gift items, a museum of Roycroft curios of all sorts, and possibly more. There are many supernatural tales about this building (formerly "The Copper Shop", used in Hubbard's original Roycroft metalworking operation). The most persuasive comes to us from the 70's.

The police told the owners of a break-in at the Gift Shop. The alarm had gone off in their station just three blocks away. (It was "Sonitrol," which records the sounds inside when the alarm is tripped.) Officers and employees ringed the small shop.

It was a late fall night. An inch or two of new snow about the building was totally unmarked. No one had left the Gift Shop in several hours. Police and Roycrofters went in and found furniture moved, but nobody home. They were dumbfounded. Back at the station, the tape made no mistake: it had caught footsteps.

SHADOW OF THE SERVING GIRL

Many old Roycroft houses and barns are scattered throughout the village of East Aurora. One of our best stories comes from some apartments over on Prospect Avenue, the former Emerson Hall (home of unmarried women working at Roycroft).

The storyteller - a bright, well-adjusted young man employed at Fisher-Price - had once attended one of the author's lectures on paranormal phenomena. A year or so later he reported being troubled by something he had seen a few nights before. Someone had touched him in his apartment, waking him from a sound sleep. A woman in antique clothing was in the room. There was something strange about her appearance; she clearly didn't belong there. "Get out of here!" he shouted, frightened. "Leave me alone!" After a lingering, cool glance, she faded out.

He was troubled by the affair. We reminded him of the deep questioning we should all have about paranormal experiences; he seemed convinced he had seen something. So we consoled him as a Spiritualist might. This was, after all, a fairly natural spook to be seen in a building like this, once the home of working women. It was not out of place, as if it were a demon sent after him alone.

THE MIDNIGHT CORSAIR

One of the Inn's former handymen is a crusty chap who thrives on "getting a rise" out of people. One would think he would be first in line with a provocative tale like this one from the late sixties, but it took some pushing to get him to speak his piece. He had nothing to make of his own single brush with the indefinable.

In the early 90's we first asked the handyman what he knew about the paranormal lore of the Inn. He said he knew nothing and had heard nothing. We were given the outlines of this story a year or so afterward by a fellow-witness - the tale's other mortal actor - who insisted this former handyman could tell far more of it than he. To the handyman we returned. Why, we asked, had he told us nothing the first time? Because, he replied, he did not want everyone to think he was crazy. They do already, we reassured him. He blinked, seemed to brighten with agreement, and told his tale.

He began with the only thing he had ever heard about Roycroft supernaturalism before his own encounter with it: the rumor that, on rainy nights, "the ghost of Elbert Hubbard might return." A resident of the Inn during its flophouse days, he concedes that on this fateful late night he had been "overserved" with spirits of the bottled kind. In the middle of the night he went to the lavatory down the hall and saw one of his floormates in a doorway, aghast. Not far down the dim hall, with the aura of unreality about it, was the image of a man in a white shirt with the sleeves rolled up and a sword - a rapier - in his hand. This was a longhaired, solidly built man the handyman sensed must be Elbert Hubbard. This figure was just walking purposefully down the hall.

Our storyteller used the facilities according to plan, and when he emerged no swordsman was about. Yet the next morning he found his hall-mate of the night before pointing up to the ceiling. The old foil depended from it, half its shaft embedded in the soft, light insulating panels. He gave it to another employee who made far more of it than he did. This coworker left the area not too long after, and so far as the handyman knows, the sword is with him still.

HUB'S MYSTERIOUS DEATH

Many who dig a little into Roycroft get the indefinable sense that something begs to be brought out. If founder Elbert Hubbard or others wished to keep something covered, it's probably either the occultism we have touched upon, or something relating to politics. It would either be pretty innocuous in Hubbard's day but potentially inflammatory now, or the other way around. This sense of uneasiness accompanies the circumstances around Hubbard's death.

Though his body was never found, it's a virtual certainty that Hubbard went down with the Lusitania in 1915. There would be nothing ambiguous about that had he not made references, apparently, to his own eventual death in the Irish Sea several times in the *Philistine*, once as early as 1896. Some letters that have recently surfaced - probably the last Hubbard ever wrote - feature him musing upon just that subject. In the winter of 1915 he tried to talk his wife Alice into staying in East Aurora and avoiding the fatal voyage.

What was Hubbard doing on this doomed ship? He stated that he was on his way to Europe to see for himself what was going on and to report back to the people of the United States. (He was, after all, a journalist.) This was probably true. He had a meeting with the Kaiser, apparently, which, because of Hubbard's formidable fame and connections, could probably have been arranged. Warring parties always do a lot more communicating than the general public supposes, and there was great conviction in America that World War I could be diplomatically defused. Prominent citizens - particularly capitalists like Henry Ford - felt called upon to head over and see what they could do. It was a far different thing than mixing with Hitler a quarter of a century later.

There are several recollections of "The Fra's" last moments with his beloved wife. One witness maintains that they stood on the bow for awhile, observing the chaotic tragedy and yielding their spots in the lifeboats to others. Then, hand in hand, they went back to their stateroom, awaiting the end.

Another story has them scrambling like the rest inside a lifeboat, still attached to the ship, high over the waves. A rope broke before the boat could be lowered to the water, spilling its preppies into the cool drink. For all but those hardy enough to swim the seven miles to Ireland, death would have been inevitable.

A third impression spots Hubbard last on the bow of the ship, saluting the parting lifeboats and going down with it in that position. That's our favorite, so characteristic of the earthly Hubbard - never a military man - ending his earthly life with a gesture grand, stoic, and altruistic, but also just a bit off.

Yet still another story puts him on the shores of Ireland, dapper, unruffled, and inquiring about his wife among a group of survivors. As for why he failed to reenter the world of affairs, the teller of the tale has no explanations. It's little wonder there are different versions; the scene itself was confusion's masterpiece. But other questions are unanswered.

Why was Hubbard going to Germany? Did he forecast his death? The conspiracy club would have a field day with either. Germany has been a hotbed of secret philosophical groups and sinister accusation since the Renaissance; and a man who writes about ageless wizards, dabbles in occultism, predicts his own death, and then seems to go to it raises red flags in many imaginations.

But we digress. One final wrinkle is in the mix. The spot of the Lusitania's sinking is on or very near a global alignment of geomantic significance, which appears also to go through Western New York. For this, the reader is invited to turn to the final chapter, "The Dragon Path."

MAGNA MATER

"GREAT TRAVAIL IS CREATED FOR EVERY MAN FROM THE DAY HE GOES OUT OF HIS MOTHER'S WOMB TO THE DAY THAT HE RETURNS TO THE MOTHER OF ALL THINGS."

TEN MODERN SPOOKS

MARTHA MATHEWSON

A ghost may come;
For it is a ghost's right,
His element is so fine
Being sharpened by his death
To drink from the wine-breath
While our gross palates drink from the whole wine.

W. B.Yeats

TWENTIETH-CENTURY HAUNTINGS

The iconography of the modern imagination is, as many observe, not totally different from that of centuries past. The same old mythic patterns at least occasionally recycle themselves. A sword will probably always have a more clear-cut inner significance than an Uzi or a phaser. So, perhaps, will a spook.

Spook lore is alive and well, no matter how many of us have computers and surf the internet; those who doubt it need only do a little freelance interviewing of their own about the Western Door. We could have had five hundred ghost stories by now if all that mattered was individual hearsay. We were interested in patterns, though, of sites and events that had wide testimony and at least a measure of the other possible evidence available. It may seem a little dull, but eight of the sites and events we picked have been written about many times, six of them in national publications. Only two are our discoveries.

We have trouble suspending our disbelief. We consider it possible that much, most, or all we have been told in the way of modern ghost stories is illusion - imagination, more or less waking dreams, sincerely believed. The rest could be outright whoppers. We never suspend our curiosity, though. We also consider the possibility that paranormal experience may sometimes be real.

In some modern cases, there is more to go on than mere verbal testimony. Twentieth century folk may be no more truthful than those of the nineteenth (and no less superstitious), but they're more apt to consider other explanations before presuming they've seen a ghost. Also, modern technology occasionally catches something curious. A few of those cases are ahead.

A word should be added, though, about "haunted" sites, since in every case these listed are still with us. These reports have been compiled across decades; here they're stacked into two-page articles. Suggestion, gossip, and impressionability are everyday companions, but true paranormal experience, if it exists at all, seems terribly rare. Were every surveillance gadget imaginable at work in every corner of each storied site, we would be surprised at two unexplained observations in a calendar year. Paranormal experience may be like murder (which tends to stymie witnesses, too): it may happen only infrequently, maybe even once, at a single place, when it's unexpected and hardest to prove. There may also be "high-crime" places where it happens more frequently; there's no guarantee it will when those most interested in observing it are by. Enjoy the tales; do not count on them to re-enact themselves for your visit.

THE STRANGE CASE OF
SASSAFRAS CHARLEY

The papers were on fire with it: "Supernatural Murder!" Her twelve-year-old son had found Clothilde Marchand, wife of a famous artist, dead in their Buffalo home one March afternoon in 1930. Within twenty-four hours two Cayuga women from the Cattaraugus Reservation (near Gowanda) had admitted to the killing at the behest of a Cayuga mystic known as "Sassafras Charley." He was unavailable for questioning, however; he had died weeks before.

Sassafras Charley Bowen had been a familiar figure to many Buffalonians. He sold trinkets, charms, herbs, his own nifty whittling, and, of course, sassafras. To his mostly Seneca neighbors he was a Cayuga, and somewhat offbeat. Sassafras Charley was into the firewater, too, which most people felt accounted for his bad moments - including the practice of sorcery. The rite he performed in front of a cabin of Christian Senecas (one of several deeds that got him into hot water) would probably never have been discovered but for the aftereffects - some red powder he had sprinkled in the snow outside. Several young Seneca threw Sassafras Charley off the reservation and stood guard over the cabin a few nights thereafter.

Charley's death had been hard on his sixty-six-year-old widow Nancy, a Cayuga herbalist and healer. It was she whose hammer-blows had killed the artist's wife. Her twentysomething co-conspirator Lila Jimerson - half-Seneca, half-Cayuga - was accounted a seer, even the inheritor of some of Charley's magic after he passed into the dateless night. The Bowens' close friend Lila had been a model for Henri Marchand, the illustrator at the Buffalo Museum of Natural Sciences. She rode with him around Buffalo as his wife was being killed.

In the weeks before the murder, Jimerson and Bowen had received letters (never traced to any mortal hand) naming Mrs. Marchand as a "White witch" whose long-range maleficence was behind many reservation deaths. An escalating series of messages from the beyond were arriving through Lila (in a number of occult methods), attesting even that it was Mrs. Marchand who had killed Sassafras Charley. For weeks the two women had been aiming traditional Six Nations magic at Clothilde Marchand. Its failure must have convinced them of her sorcerous power. The final stroke - a ouija board message from Sassafras Charley - might have pushed others over the edge.

The Jimerson-Bowen trial may not have sensitized the public to Iroquois issues, but it woke them up to the supernaturalism on the reservation. Though there were many Christian Seneca, Handsome Lake's Longhouse religion was strong, encouraging the old Six Nations traditions (in which wizardry was an active agent). One "expert" testified that an Iroquois would kill his best friend if convinced this was the source of a hex. The sober scholar Arthur C. Parker agreed that the Six Nations took magic for real.

Henri Marchand was a man of suave Gallic manners and great prestige. The papers presumed he was devoted to his family and his work of painting on the Cattaraugus Reservation, where Marchand had many acquaintances. He'd driven his models - among them Lila Jimerson - to various sites. Many Whites concluded that his wife's murder was moved by infatuation: thinking to marry her husband, Lila Jimerson had Mrs. Marchand killed. It was more complicated than that.

As time and trial went on, Marchand was thoroughly tarnished. A Buffalo paper printed some letters he had written to Lila Jimerson; artist and model had long been more than friends, and Marchand had lied to the police about it. He'd had affairs with more Iroquois women than he could count and more women of all types than he could reliably estimate. He lived the image of the Continental artist, and his Continental wife (if so she expected to remain) was expected to understand.

When chided on the stand about his infidelities, Marchand claimed that he needed clear impressions of the Iroquois women's breasts for his displays. (A nubile and hopefully accurate little image still in one of Marchand's dioramas is said to represent Lila.) Iroquois women did not show themselves to men with whom they were not intimate, thus Marchand's seductions of them served art. [The reaction to this line in the real Buffalo courtroom can only rival that of the Pink Panther's filmed one - abrupt laughter - as "Inspector Closeau" (Peter Sellers), when asked how his family could live luxuriously on his policeman's salary, deadpanned that his wife (a jewel-thief unbeknownst) was frugal with the laundry money.]

Occult speculation lent a lurid cast to the newspaper accounts, but it was not the focus of legal matters. Shouts of racism and conspiracy from the women's defenders would be familiar in the late 1990's. Caught between state and federal authorities (who sent a formidable team to defend the women), the case became a lightning rod for issues of cross-cultural communication, Native American sovereignty, and the role of religion in it all. Even jury selection was hard, because many prospective jurors refused to consider the death penalty for a woman. It was, after all, a charge of premeditated murder.

It's hard to form a conviction about the case and the virtual acquittal of the two women. No one doubted that they'd committed the murder, but they were let off with no more punishment than the ordeal of the trials. Maybe the jury regarded the women as so uneducated and superstitious that they knew not what they did; maybe it felt the real culprit was not on trial.

The all-male jury seems to have loathed Marchand's amorous escapades and sensed it no one else's fault that something finally blew up. They may even have suspected that Marchand had a hand in provoking the murder. (There were those mysterious letters.) The artist did not flatter his image, having taken another wife - eighteen years old - by the time of the verdicts in 1931. Then again, the jury may have come to believe that the spirit of a Cayuga shaman had driven two women to the murder of one. We grieve for Clothilde, wife, mother, and undoubted victim. The injustices dealt her are not unclear.

FAUSTUS AT THE EASTMAN

"What there is about the Genesee Valley of upper New York State to invite witches, I don't know," wrote Paul Horgan in April 1936 (*Harper's* magazine). He goes on to assess the pastoral landscape - tame rivers, green hills, and modest architecture - and allude to Rochester's reputation for occultism. He reflects back to the mid-1800's and the mysterious rappings - the "Rochester Knockings" - that followed the Fox sisters to their stay in that city, that even supplanted, in the popular mind, the originals from their Hydesville hometown. Perhaps he ponders the tales about the Mt. Hope Cemetery and the Ontario coastline, or the lively cycles about Rochester's Corn Hill and Paddy Hill. Maybe he knows, as he writes, more than he tells; but his story is his own experience at the Eastman Theater.

It was a chance shipboard conversation in 1923 between George Eastman and a certain Monsieur Vladimir Rosing - director, entrepreneur, and musician - that led to the birth of the Eastman Theater. "Val" Rosing was also more or less of an impresario whose vision courted (and married) Eastman's cash, and who, by midwinter of 1924 (during the brief flourishing called "The Rochester Renaissance") was preparing Gounod's *Faust,* a devilish work if ever there was.

One night in that long winter a number of the company held a seance for the after-rehearsal relaxation. The apartment of Rosing's fiance Peggy Williamson was the site, and eight living souls (including author Horgan) attended. A big old mahogany table (with griffins' claw legs) was the support for the hand-holding, and the means by which the spook rapped his word.

From the sounds of things, this was a seance from the century before. The heavy table did a virtual jig, lifting one side up to six inches off the floor, tapping and banging to indicate yes or no. Through this cumbersome means the Rochester spook announced himself as "Faustus," perhaps in honor of the grim play they were all performing. Needless to say, this was unsettling. One of the most thematic figures in European literature, Faustus had been a Medieval doctor who sold his soul to the devil for knowledge and power. Somewhere between Marlowe and Goethe he reached his highest literary personification. Surely this contact from a spook claiming to be the real thing must have terrified the roomful of actors, especially when we consider the superstition surrounding *Macbeth.* The Thane of Cawdor has two brief auditions with witches; he was a piker compared to Faust, who does business with their boss.

The Rochester Faustus was as melodramatic as a Hollywood genie, pounding portents like "Life is of the soul, and secret," and "Words die on the edge of your world." This suggests to us that many of these utterances came from the unconscious minds of the people in attendance; but it proves only that detached human essences, upon joining the choir invisible, do not all become poets.

This Faust had come back, he said, to set the record straight about his life. Knowing at least one word of Latin (in which language a medieval doctor would have been able to converse), the spook said its life had been *vanitas* (vanity), and corrected a few seemingly minor aspects of the Faust legend. It promised a display at the company's next performance.

The story made the rounds, but there was still no explanation for what happened on the appointed day. A cross of light appeared on the stage floor and began to flick and dance about, in full view of the audience, which included George Eastman. It vanished, and no one knew how it had come to move as it had. The light-room had been vacant.

This incident may be modest (like most paranormal effects), and it would seem a lot more impressive had this exact deed been foretold by the entity "Faustus," or had his calling-card been more enduring. Yet the light crew could not explain the prodigy. Conviction ran through the cast that, this time, they had messed with something they should have left alone.

More recent lore would have it that the Eastman is haunted by two apparitions: the ghost of a young woman named Catherine who threw herself off the balcony of the theater, and that of Mr. George Eastman himself, who sometimes appears in his regular seat - number 48. No word yet if the other ghost lands on him.

BONNIE'S FIFTH DEV

There might be a couple of reasons that a ghost story is not unusual on this campus. St. Bonaventure is a very religious place, and thoughts of the spiritual and other-worldly are never far from it. And college students, whether or not they are as superstitious as actors, are surely on the eager lookout for spectacular tales. One of the best-known haunted sites among the college set of the Western Door is the fifth floor of St. Bonaventure's Devereaux Hall.

Nicknamed "Fifth Dev" by the Bonnies, this is a residence hall that was constructed sometime in the 1800's. It's one of the older buildings on campus, and students joke that the administration keeps its exact age secret to minimize groaning about its amenities. In the mid-1960's, a handful of students got hold of some occult texts and decided to do a black mass on the top floor, whose single room is like a big attic, with plenty of dormers. The students stole some unconsecrated hosts, drew their circle and pentagram, and had a dark old time of it. At that point, our sources tell us, nothing paranormal happened. Yet word of the matter leaked to the administration. Some students were kicked out; then the fun started.

Persistent reports of paranormal effects have deviled the fifth floor ever since: lights, footsteps noticeable to those beneath, signs of activity when the place is vacant - the usual run. The place is simply cursed, say others. It has long been the site of private natural parties, as well as typical student wackiness. The supernatural rep of "Fifth Dev" did nothing but enhance its recreational utility.

Talk to the students at St. Bonaventure and you'll find that the tales about Fifth Dev are still in force. Of course they have all the trappings of folklore of everywhere else, and one can see that to some degree this cycle is propagating itself. Very often a whole round of rumors will get started over some easily-quelled supposition - reports of mysterious lights within the troubled space, for instance, when they are quite surely simple reflections from a landing or hall. The trouble is (as in so many troublesome cases) that there seem to be so many witnesses at the root.

It's not often that events in the practical world seem to confirm suppositions from the realms of impression; the matter of "Fifth Dev" may be one of them. The fifth floor of Devereaux Hall is still empty and unused, though the university has built new housing since. (One would think it would first fill all the space it has.) Our sources tell us "Fifth Dev" was only used as living space in a pinch, so its current vacancy is nothing strange. Still, "Something to do with insurance" is all the explanation we have heard for its fallow state.

THE HOUSE ON THE POINT

[Where the Cattaraugus meets Lake Erie near Silver Creek and the ancient trail that became Route 5 is a tender bay between two rocky fingers - another piece of Spirit Way real estate with more than its measure of folklore. We'll keep the specs to ourselves, since the house on the point may not really be "haunted." These are the rumors.]

A century ago the port city Buffalo was one of the glamour spots on the lakes. Its stylish families made their summer homes - many of them virtual estates - along this road that flanks the shore of the southeastern Erie. One of them, according to the rumors, may still not be at its ease.

There's been plenty of history here, some of it gloomy. There were engagements about the mouth of the Cattaraugus in all three of the early American wars. A British warship in the last conflict chased some smaller American vessels into it and opened fire. An archaeological team reported apparitions and odd sound effects on the banks of this creek as they worked. Melodic, ancient chanting seems to be carried on the still air of warm twilights. A burial mound near the creek was exposed by the water, and bones were carried into the lake. A remarkable artifact - a pipe in the shape of a mastodon - was found near here, dating from the last Ice Age.

Trauma was associated with the area for a long time, according to the Native Americans. We know the Eries - the "Cat" Tribe - were extinguished as a cultural group by the Iroquois in the 1650's. The war was by all accounts a sprawling affair, and one of its climactic engagements was likely near here. LaSalle's ship the *Griffin* may have gone aground near here around 1679, losing its crew to marauding Seneca. We sense there's something deeper that our Seneca sources could not recall - or would not tell us.

There's a promontory, a high rocky finger soaring an impressive mansion out above the choppy lake. Something is off about it. Many sites about the Western Door - the Pink House, Fort Niagara, the Van Horn Mansion - appear in national texts on the paranormal and the strange. The supernatural reputation of the house on the point is new even to the local historians; but a wide variety of people who have lived near it and worked in it are in no doubt.

Even its physical environment is off. The outside is graceful; the inside is rough, almost rustic. Rooms have been closed off and a door in the basement wall never opened. Some days in steamy summer the huge fireplace blazes, and the heat is on. Still, people wear heavy coats and sweaters inside. Under the best of circumstances, there are perpetual cold spots - a trademark of paranormal sites.

Even the current owners - who are having none of the supernaturalism - confirm the death, back in the early parts of this century. The builder of the virtual palace was a factory owner; a young woman died in an upstairs bedroom that seems to be the nexus of the lore. Mysterious lights have been seen in and near this room from other spots in the house. Once a part of it was sealed off behind a new wall. From a spot in this room there is a very odd natural sound effect: sometimes when the window is open and boaters in the bay are in just the right spot, fifty feet below and hundreds out, one can hear them as clearly as if they were in the yard.

Whatever "evil" there is about the site makes itself evident to youngsters. A toddler who lived there in the eighties was prone to odd, symbolically self-destructive gestures, like stringing leashes and clotheslines about his neck, mimicking a hanging. It was only when his own personality began to form that he outgrew the baleful influence. Children also have seen many apparitions, including that of an aged watchman with his distinctive lantern.

The whole point is cursed, in the words of a longtime resident. According to a story that comes to us in several versions, even the Church (at the request of a neighbor) got involved with the house. Apparently, its influences were making themselves evident to a mother who feared for her children. Some religious action was taken out here, possibly the burying of amulets about the troubled house.

The haunted point seems also to project its influence in natural, though strange, ways. Situations that would almost never develop any-where else seem to develop here. One instance that comes to mind concerns a normally stable retired businessman from a discrete family who returned with an axe to an outdoor summer party to resume an argument. (His intent can only be surmised, since the tool was instantly confiscated by the six-foot six-inch former mayor of Orchard Park.) Another concerns an eccentric old woman who lived on the tiny road leading to the cliff above the water. Surreally devoted to her motley passle of dogs, she died or passed out during a seizure. When her body was found a day or so later it had been partially eaten by her own brood. Neither episode is supernatural; both suggest the general sense of unrest typical of paranormally troubled sites.

PHANTOM OF THE PFEIFER

[Actors may be a superstitious bunch, but other witnesses - managers, technicians, administrators - attest to the strange events at Buffalo's Pfeifer Theater. We thank members of the staff, eager - as are we - to solve mysteries.]

In the Prohibition Era, Buffalo was known as the state's hottest stop outside New York City. Twenty-four hours a day, every day, somewhere in the city something - music, vaudeville, gambling, drinking - was going on. The old Town Supper Club - later the Town Casino - wasn't the biggest public venue, but it was the hippest.

Many famous entertainers were here: Red Skelton, Cab Calloway, Sammy Davis, Jr., Burns & Allen, Edgar Bergen and Charlie McCarthy, and Johnny Mathis. They say this Main Street speakeasy was Al Capone's favorite Buffalo hangout. High rollers walking on the wild side rolled into all sorts of prohibited activities. The Town Supper Club had the best food, the finest booze, the slinkiest show girls, and an aura of intrigue. In recent decades the building has alternated vacancy and use as the Studio Arena Theater. Owned by the University of Buffalo for about the last fifteen years, the building now thrives as the Pfeifer Theater.

There are a number of physical reasons for the Pfeifer to seem curious. Its passages twist and turn. Old safes have never been opened, and tunnel-mouths in its walls are bricked-up. The modern stage - virtually a building within a building - has a cavernous feel, and samples of the original architecture sprout from the bare old walls through the new.

Three tunnels beneath the building were allegedly used during the Prohibition Era: one ran all the way to the Peace Bridge (for smuggling booze); one reached the water (for sneaking in immigrant labor); and another went right to City Hall (we won't guess). When the NFTA tracks were laid outside the Pfeifer's door, the builders found such a honeycomb of tunnels that Main Street was likely to collapse if there was any more burrowing. Rumors of the "Underground Railroad" follow any old house or subterranean space about Western New York; they do likewise with these tunnels beneath Main Street and the Pfeifer Theater.

It's easy to know when you're alone in the Pfeifer; its alarm system checks every part of it for motion. It's also easy to know when an experience - a sight, a sound, an object moving - should have no natural cause. The Pfeifer certainly seems an active site, but the folklore links its effects to no specific source, certainly no single ghost. Things happen, and people report them, usually with gusto. Apparitions (which also vary widely) are encountered by people alone or in small groups. Sometimes the image is just a shadow moving across a light source or darting at the end of a passage. Sometimes it's a face in an aperture at various spots in the theater, and sometimes a whole person who soon disappears. Employees have resigned over such instances, some even rushing from the building with lights and appliances still on.

Sound effects seem prominent at the Pfeifer Theater, some of them of staggering violence. Inanimate sounds (like heavy vault doors slamming) are reported. Heavy footsteps are described, and voices are heard, either single or many. In the latter case the effect is like walking by a party in full swing, almost as if someone was replaying the sounds of its Prohibition-era heyday. Someone heard a dog barking deep underground, seemingly in one of the tunnels behind the wall. Once even a phantom vacuum cleaner was heard at work. The Pfeifer seems to hold some immaterial tape recorder that occasionally plays itself back.

The same casual charge cannot be made of the Pfeifer's physical effects. While we can't make the case for an out-and-out infestation of poltergeists, something out of the ordinary seems occasionally afoot. Once some stage-daggers were moved several feet and arranged in a pattern in the darkness, minutes after the building's only occupant set them down. Pranks have been played in out-of-the-way places; high lights were realigned, and a metal fixture against the ceiling removed, both overnight. The ladder needed for such feats was heavy, hard to move, and in storage. In such circumstances, it takes less labor to blame supernatural agents than mortal conspiracies.

A "cold spot," seems unimpressive to the casual observer, but it's a common effect about the classic paranormal site. The Pfeifer would seem to have several. Those who walk through them often have strong emotional reactions, as if entering a psychological experience as well as a climatic one.

The many seemingly unrelated effects at the Pfeifer Theater conform more to our picture of the paranormal than to the one in popular impression (in which a ghost is always behind the matter). We've visited a lot of allegedly paranormal sites and talked to hundreds of people. We've never felt sure that there was a supernatural identity behind apparently supernatural effects. It's all a mystery. That goes double at the Pfeifer.

FREDONIA'S IGOE HALL

He so anticipated the fall of 1970, this congenial young man never to see it. After his freshman year at Fredonia State University, he and his friends from Alumni Hall - among them Louis Szczukowski - were planning to be neighbors again in a dorm so new their wing was called merely "Hall E." A big lake had other plans.

The morning after the Fourth of July, Fredonia sophomore-to-be Lou Szczukowski woke with a feeling we all know - a sense of disturbance that makes no sense, like "someone walking on your shadow." Soon after, Lou found out what it was: his friend and suite-mate Jimmy Igoe had drowned in the treacherous Erie. His body was missing several days.

A quarter of a century later, Lou Szczukowski is a Public Safety officer at his alma mater. A strong, good-natured, no-nonsense man, he gives with a touch of sadness the natural elements of the story. Supernatural ones come to us from many others.

In September of 1970, many of the friends of Jimmy Igoe were living where he would have in the new dorm's Hall E. When the student body was polled for names for the unchristened wings, some predictable ones (for the early '70's) came up. Shultz Hall is named for "Peanuts" cartoonist Charles, Hendrix Hall for guitarist Jimi, Hemingway for writer Ernest, and the like. Up also came Igoe, and so Jimmy's never-to-be residence was named.

Even that autumn many of the students noticed strange doings around the dorm. The first displays involved an elevator that seemed to run itself, opening frequently and spontaneously on the floor where Jimmy's closest friends lived. They attributed this to "a few bugs in the system," and joked that Jimmy was along for the ride. "Hi, Jimmy!" they called out merrily to anything unexplained.

Jimmy Igoe had been set to move into the 201 suite, near the malfunctioning elevator. Reports make this area a nexus for strange occurrences, and portray the Hall itself still suffering from a leisurely infestation of poltergeists. A Campus Center director and former Igoe Hall supervisor testified that, during a conversation with a student in this hall, two mirrors fell to the floor spontaneously and shattered. One student wishing to remain anonymous told a reporter that things in his room seemed to move on their own. A director of the hall reported in *The Leader* (the school paper) that a roomful of male students were nearly in tears when their full soda cans rose in the air in front of them. When the resident jesters of Chautauqua Hall stole the portrait of Jimmy Igoe, paranormal "chaos erupted." They took it back the next day.

So far as we know, no one has reported the image of Jimmy Igoe anywhere but in the fabled painting. Why the student body links a poltergeist with their departed fellow is anybody's guess, but it's probably unfair. Much the way actors fear saying the name "Macbeth" outside a theater lest they forget and say it inappropriately within one (bringing serious bad luck), some Fredonia students are afraid to say anything about the mystery of Igoe Hall or even the living Jimmy, lest that, perhaps, draw further manifestations. Yet others can be whimsical about the matter. A *Leader* article boasts a wry list (a la the 1990's David Letterman TV show) of the top ten reasons that Jimmy Igoe still haunts his hall. Ah, is nothing sacred? Not to college students, apparently, which is probably as it should be. Respect can be a gesture, granted under compulsion; reverence is a sentiment, and the capacity to feel it comes with life-experience. We revere the young life cut short. May our mention of the prominent tale add nothing to the grief of those whose loss this was.

ERINN MCELHANEY

SMOKESTACKS AND SHAMROCKS

[Currently in dry dock near Buffalo harbor as part of the Naval and Military Park, The USS The Sullivans is listed in national directories of haunted places.]

One of the greatest tragedies that ever befell any American family fell upon the Sullivans (of Waterloo, Iowa) in World War Two. In 1942 the five Sullivan brothers were aboard their light cruiser (the USS Juneau) when it was attacked off the coast of Guadalcanal Island. Ten out of the hundreds survived, but not one of the brothers Sullivan. The Navy named a ship in the brothers' memory.

Legend has it that by midnight of every Friday the thirteenth, the Sullivan brothers will revisit the ship named for them and leave a calling card - a demonstration of their presence. Few of the members of "The USS The Sullivans Association" (more or less the alumni of the fabled ship) doubt the rumors.

In November of 1992, *Buffalo News* columnist Bob Curran wrote about the ship. He had met a man who had served on the USS The Sullivans in its last few years of active duty, a balanced individual who stressed that he was not superstitious; then he confided in Curran that strange things often did seem to happen every Friday the thirteenth. On his first watch aboard the ship, someone had polished just one of the names - George - on the plaque commemorating the Sullivan brothers. The man knew such a gesture was not part of the regular duty, and considered some paranormal explanation likeliest. Maybe this was George's turn to manifest.

Other rumors involve the sounds of a ghostly craps game and voices whispering, "Hey you!" Apparitions include five floating forms, seeming to walk on air, and even a grisly burned specter, reported in 1993 by a security guard. Electrical pranks are commonly reported of paranormal sites, and they occur at this one, too.

The tragedy of the Sullivans spurred the Navy to its current practice of separating brothers. No American family will again be so affected by a single stroke delivered to a single ship. The shamrocks on its stacks and the name on its sides may not be all this one gives us to commemorate the brothers Sullivan.

THE VANISHING
HITCHHIKER REVISITED

["The Vanishing Hitchhiker" is such a prominent figure of modern gossip that it's even been made the title of a book (by Jan Harold Brunvand) on urban folklore. Most of us have heard such a tale; "The Choking Doberman" and "The Lovers' Stalled Car" are others. These stories are always delivered third-hand, and they always happen to an acquaintance of someone the storyteller knows. Seldom if ever can they be traced to a single, verifiable source. (The pros have tried.) We hope by indulging the subject we are not "falling for it" again, but the quality of some of the stories from the Buffalo and Rochester areas seems a little different from the simple campfire tale. In the variants that have roused our interest, there are eyewitnesses who do not fear to testify in print.]

Sometimes she's a little girl, wet, wretched and lonely. A man driving up Delaware Avenue on a clammy night sees her weeping and drenched on a Tonawanda cemetery bench, in tattered clothing. "I'm cold and hungry and tired," she replies to his query, "and have so far to go." She gives him an address in the City of Tonawanda; she climbs into his car and snuggles into the upholstery. He talks cheerfully; she is quiet. "Here we are," he calls heartily when they arrive at the house. Of course, nobody is beside him. Over the next few months he learns that a girl matching her description had lived at the same house. She had died years before, and was buried in the cemetery near which he had first spotted her.

Sometimes she's a little old woman, frazzled, peeved, and obsessed with some emergency. At two o'clock one rainy morning a man, his wife, and their baby were driving north on Delaware Avenue. As they neared Forest Lawn Cemetery, a little old woman stepped into their headlights, waving her arms in the glare. She gave them an address, got in the back seat of their car, and even talked. She pointed out the house as they came down her street. When the car stopped and they turned around to look... No one. Astonished, they rang the bell. They described the woman to the owner, who said she sounded like his dead wife, and that other people had had the same experience. The driver was troubled enough to tell the story to the Buffalo police.

Sometimes, she's a little sinister. In 1924 in Chautauqua County she was a "strange apparition" hailing streetcars and disappearing when they stopped. In Lockport she is an old woman haunting Cold Springs Road near a one-lane bridge over a small creek. Sometimes she disappears when the late-night motorists stop for her. Sometimes she accepts a ride, hoping to get to her home. She disappears as they go over the bridge, right from in between two people. [We remember the old superstition that the children of the left hand - witches, fairies, and vampires - cannot cross thresholds (even symbolic ones like running water) of their own accord. They must be ferried - or invited.]

Sometimes he is a longhaired, bearded young man, oddly clothed (some say robed), often seen on the I-90 between Erie and Rochester. The

State Police get reports about this one. He rants from the back seat, makes predictions, and storms forth upon the ills of the modern world like an Old Testament prophet the week before the Second Coming. He vanishes without unfastening his seat belt.

Folklore in itself has meaning, even if its tales are not literally true. We cannot help but think the story of the vanishing hitchhiker has some reason for being. There are too many eyewitnesses. Are they all liars? Yet the last of the versions above might be one we can to lay to rest with no question mark on its tombstone.

We'd say that the scruffy, preaching male figure that started that cycle of these tales could have been the author himself in his college days. Then he had a lot more hair, frequently took to the thumb to get himself up the '90, felt greatly smarter than he does today, and remembers being vastly more prone to telling other people how to solve their problems... except for the vanishing part. Can't remember how we did that one.

THE HOLE TO HELL

[This Hinsdale site is pretty famous about the foothills of the Appalachians, but we won't help you find it.]

A handful of hunting cabins brood from still higher over the house in the queer hilltop depression. It's old, though, as far as we can tell, the rumors - and the haunting - are strictly modern. An old coach stop, they say, on burial grounds of the Seneca, the site of a family's massacre. Add the seventies shotgun suicide of a Vietnam vet and teenagers who drove into the pond, ending life in its chill clutches.

The old-timers shake their heads. It may have been an old coach stop, but no massacre took place. In the mid-1970's it was the site of a haunting so violent and public that it even made the papers, and, through the satanism scare of the early-80's, a hell-Mecca for legions of adolescents, on late nights in all stages of intoxication; little wonder if some came to trouble. None of this, however, the young man knew before moving in in the early 1980's. To this former football star and father of four small girls, the old farm house and pond seemed too good to be true.

His first sign of trouble came five minutes into the unloading. A neighbor - a retired FBI man - came up and said, "Are you crazy?" He expounded as passionately as he could about the psychic dangers of the place. The young father didn't believe a word. In the basement he saw the pentagram from a satanic mass the night before.

The next step in the escalating play involved the attitudes of the living. The biggest family dog was a selfless protector of children, the father's beloved companion on many a hunt and hike on foot or skis. A wolf-shepherd-husky mix that had previously feared nothing, she forfeited her usual post by the girls and would not enter the house at night, even in winter.

The young father grew more alone. His children became airily distant as if, among the trees, were private playmates more stylish and charming than anyone knew. Almost before he noticed, the airy suburban gypsy he had married - tie-dyes and sunny spirits - now paced like a Brontë heroine in long somber dresses. When she came in from her walks by pond and wood, it seemed she'd been talking to someone.

Rumors surfaced by the week. It was custom for teachers from the local school to visit families for a conference; none would come to this house. Carloads of high-schoolers came uninvited. Bane or magnet, the site was widely regarded as a source of power which, the young father suspected, was targeting him.

For months, the oil heat system shut down precisely as he came home from work. (The fuel company couldn't figure it out.) For another spell, the young father was scalded in the middle of every shower; the water just turned hot. He kept resetting the heat, but could never settle the problem (which bedeviled no one else).

There were other effects. A wood stove converted to propane often geysered foot-high flames. A hanging picture slanted awry of its own accord. Flies swarmed a room near the attic. A strange, small moving light - seemingly timed to the flaring stove - set off two smoke alarms as it neared them and may have been caught on film by a research team. Its source seemed to be the attic. At times the house was permeated by an overpowering, unexplained perfume, widely taken as a sign of the murdered mother (whose daughter was often spotted in old dresses, in nearby fields). The woman of the house heard a little girl repeatedly calling from outside. At first she thought it was her own daughters. They were inside.

This camel's back broke from two straws. "Some ground is just bad," a minister finally said. "No one knows why. Just leave as soon as you can, and take only your own things with you. Don't discuss your plans inside the house. That place is just a hole to Hell." Yet worse was coming.

On one of those last spring days, the family's biggest dog, heavy with puppies, leaped from the porch beside the girls and dashed under her master's moving truck, snuffing many lives in a second. As he stood staring, searching for answers, the unborn pups kicked inside her. She had known what a truck was. What could have called her before it? "This place killed that dog," he said when he could speak.

The last night was a virtual Walpurgisnacht. When their grandmother came for the children, the electric locks of her car malfunctioned, working normally again only miles from the cursed hilltop. As several adults worked inside the house, the attic became an organ producing horrid sounds, a blend of windy screaming - on a windless night - and human.

Their experience left no one unchanged. Not long after, the couple went their ways. All had once seemed music and light. The young father - now a fortiesh, muscular man who can still bench three-fifty - works hard, tries to be a good man, tries to know life. He misses his daughters, he confesses, who seem to have wiped their memories of the entire experience.

Fifteen years later, the woman - once the wife whose moods had changed so much - is near a loss to describe her former self, but becomes a poet in the attempt. Her eyes light. She never slept better than there, as troubled as her husband was. She never dreamt, and often woke to find him up protectively, a shotgun on his lap. Even as she grew away from him, she feared that one time he would not return from one of his nightly swims in their pond.

Whatever energy was about the spot was female, she felt, perhaps connected to the mother and daughter said to be murdered there. She grew in it by the day, as if joining something wondrous and natural for the first time, gaining a joyous new aura of power. Energies coursed through her like an inner life as that outside her became coincidental. Like a dream of flying in which the only trick is to believe, it seemed only time before she became like her effortless, invisible tutors. The first steps were already clear. She looked hard at vases and clock faces, and even saw their first movements to her will. What lay ahead! She was loath to leave. She wonders at it all now.

WAIF BETWEEN WORLDS

[A modern Holiday Inn seems to lack the atmosphere of the classic haunted building. We would agree, except that the one essential component is the spook - and it seems Grand Island has a fine one.]

Her name, they say, is Tanya, the spectral little girl of five or six whose favorite place is Room 422. Some who spot her vividly describe her high-button black shoes and red dress from the century before. For others she comes more shyly, in the shades and shadows typical of our images of ghosts. She seems to be, in a word, childish.

It may be Tanya playing in the hotel pool after hours and disappearing before staff arrive. It may be Tanya jumping on beds in empty rooms, running through halls, and chalking odd graffiti. (Someone must be blamed for the locked, cleaned suites in disarray; the strangely playing stereos; the phone calls from vacant, unregistered rooms; the elevators coming back from the fourth floor empty.) She can be driven from a room with a rebuke, almost as if her tender feelings have been hurt. To some extent, as we see, she has adapted to the late twentieth-century's technology, but its toys still seem to fascinate her. Sometimes she wanders through the halls crying, "I'm lost." She truly seems a waif between worlds, looking for somewhere to be at home.

According to a *Buffalo Evening News* article of 1974, one of the first managers of the then year-old Inn thought Tanya was a recent invention. A maid cleaning a fourth floor room in the Inn's first month turned to see a little girl in the doorway. Something about her seemed unnatural. The maid dropped two drinking glasses, then looked up, and the girl was gone. As she tried to run out, somehow her cart trapped her in the room. She screamed.

The Grand Island Holiday Inn is an odd place for a ghost. It's a young building, and little in its background fits the stereotype of the classic paranormal site. Defying the folklore, historians can find no fire here, and no little girl who died in it the century before. (This area near Whitehaven Village was a lumbering boom town from 1834 to 1850. Grand Island had been purchased for five bucks an acre by the East Boston Company, which sent its trees horizontally to Beantown.) The environment of the Inn is not the gloomy, historic sort that puts people in mind of spooks. So why do so many stable people - guests from out of the area, unaware of the folklore - say what they say?

The lore about this Inn is some of the most convincing in the Western Door. Our favorite tale is that of the couple whose toddler's crying woke them in the night. Someone was playing with his toys. The bleary-eyed father looked to the foot of the bed, and in the dim, locked room was a strange young girl. Surprised, and suddenly very afraid, he spoke to her harshly. She withdrew, seeming to vanish as if shocked, and this may have driven her away for good.

Yet we may hold "Tanya" forever on film. (We're indebted to

Michelle Turner-Scherrer for our photos, too subtle to reproduce here.) At a fiftieth wedding anniversary celebration at the Inn, two pictures were taken of the golden couple, leaning into each other at a table littered with glasses. In the first, a cloudy shape can be seen between them, superimposed over the scene. It's hard to decipher, yet there are distinct qualities to the image: it appears to be made of white and shaded areas.

By the second picture the long-loving pair have fallen into their embrace. Right to left, the camera position is the same; it has simply elevated its focus a few degrees to better center the kiss. It's the unintended image that has moved - to the left, and into the dark space of the background. In this shot, it surely carries the impression of a spectral girl, with wild tresses and voluminous gown.

Dearest Tanya, haunting light and life and family not yours... Sleeper, dreaming in that night the other side of ours... Whoever, whatever you are, may those you come to be tender, for you mean no harm.

THE DRAGON PATH

SUE QUINBY

When the work of collecting is done, that of comparing may begin.
John Rhys

THE DRAGON PATH

[Our observations about modern geomancy are basic to the field of "Earth Mysteries," which has been explored for years by researchers such as Paul Devereux, Francis Hitching, Janet and Colin Bord, and John Michell. For our general observations of sacred architecture we owe many sources, but especially author and teacher Sig Lonegren for his insights and friendship over the years.

It was Buffalo artist Franklin LaVoie who put us onto "the Dragon Path," and without his able contributions this spine of insight would not have been available to us. For the original development, both of us are in debt to John Michell and Christine Rhone's *Twelve-tribe Nations*, the book that shows the Old World leg of "the St. Michael-Apollo Axis."]

I. THE DRAGON-FIGHT

Is there a line of force, charged with the power of the earth and symbolized in the language of ancient myth, running through the region of our familiar Western Door? The answer may take some development.

It's one of the most influential myths in the world, the battle between a culture-hero and a big snake. The World-Serpent's conflict with Scandinavian thunderer Thor ushers in Ragnarok, the end of the world's old cycle. Christian warrior-saints - like Michael and George - kill dreadful monsters that often stand for Satan (for whom "the Old Dragon" serves as an alias). Graeco-Roman myth has many dragon-strikers, but golden Perseus (killing the stony, serpent-tressed Medusa and a watery snake-beast after) may be a good example; both beasties are baneful. The Old World has too many other dragon-battles to list; their overall meaning is not so simple.

Though the Chinese dragon may be something far different, to many, the other big snakes have always been deep internal symbols associated with the powers of the earth. One might think it symbolic of the proverbial disjointedness in the Western soul - the post-industrial separation from the natural environment and all life processes - that these dragons seem fearsome. The natural force they represent appears as a danger to human society, something to be mastered, exploited, killed. Signs of the apparent soul-divide may appear even in the great books of India (often seen as a model of wholeness). Culture-hero and lightning-fighter Indra has his duel with the snaky giant Vritra, who keeps suspended all India's waters. The same mythic issue, whatever it means, may hold in the New World, in this continent, here in the Western Door.

There is an immortal tale with the dragon-fight motif from Western New York: the conflict of the Iroquois Thunder-Being Heno and the Great Horned Snake of the Niagara River, whose encounter climaxes near Niagara Falls, even shaping the earth. This is a long-developing cycle of tales, seeming critical to the heart of their mystery. Yet the Iroquois would never be linked to the Western soul-divide.

Nowhere, it seems, is there a people more connected to the earth. The simplest illustration would be to think of some of the names the

Iroquois nations had for themselves: the Mohawk were "The People of the Flint"; the Cayuga "The People from the Swamp"; the Seneca "The People of the Great Hill." Derived from the earth in their root terms for themselves, the Iroquois can hardly be said to express the disconnectedness between earth and humankind so handily charged of the industrial West. This cannot be the dragon's message.

Rather than a vengeful, animate being bent on murder, the dragon must represent a natural force in need of strategic management. It's fearful because it's awesome, awesome because it's mighty. The conflict of the demigodly hero with this beast may be harrowing and dreadful, but it is actually productive. His transfixion of the dragon with his lance (often lightning bolts) represents not the killing of a living creature, but the fixing and leashing of the force of the earth. In Europe and parts of the Americas this event is commemorated with great shrines (or mighty myths) at special spots, often representing the dragon's burial-place. The building on the strategic site may be thought to channel its energy.

II. LANDSCAPE LINES

We've talked a little bit about sacred architecture; there may be another aspect to it. Sometimes several religious sites are found along straight lines across distances of several miles. Often the aligned structures were built by different groups. (It's been known for some time that most cultures, even Christian ones, often incorporate the religious sites of earlier cultures into their own, thus maintaining whatever alignment was originally there.) This is one meaning - and the one we accept - for the word ley. (Others recognize leys also as lines of force across the landscape and even sacred pathways.) Most of them are short.

The usual rule, we believe, is still to consider four sites along the same track in ten miles as a ley. Some ley-hunters look too hard at the maps, accepting all sorts of sites besides religious ones, seeming to mark all sorts of patterns and alignments. There can't be that many, and if there are, the whole business can't mean much. Yet some major leys, we believe, are undeniable. One involving Britain's Stonehenge, Old Sarum and Salisbury Cathedral crosses about seven miles, and could hardly be accidental. The points of a grand equilateral triangle six or so miles on a side are made across the landscape by the siting of Stonehenge, Grovelly Castle, and Old Sarum (all ancient religious sites).

Many societies in the Americas had interest in straight-line paths across landscape. The Chaco Canyon culture of the American southwest and the Incas of South America give us the best-known examples of long straight trackways. Nearer the Western Door traces of a similar ancient road in Ohio were recently profiled in *Archaeology Magazine*. The sixty-mile path seemed to stretch deadly straight between Chillicothe and Newark (home of the famed serpent mound and many other conspicuous earthworks).

III. The Dragon Track

Little study of this sort has been applied to Western New York, but elsewhere, researchers have been seeking the message behind the pattern of architecture and landscape. One of the foremost is British scholar John Michell, who, with Christine Rhone and building upon the work of others, has written about what appears to be a line across Europe linking some sacred sites of the ancient world, linked also by a single theme: their consecration to dragon-fighting gods or saints. The line they name "The St. Michael-Apollo Axis" stretches with little variation from Israel's Mount Carmel through famous shrines in Greece, Italy, France, and the British Isles - 2500 miles long.

The shrines on this mighty line are some of the most conspicuous and important in Europe. These points (including the temple to Apollo at Delphi, Mont St.-Michel in France, and Skellig Michael in Ireland) only appear on the same line, however, when the curvature of the earth is counted. This might explain the late discovery of such a massive ley; most ley-hunters deal with straight-edges on short-range topo maps; bigger flat ones are inaccurate after about ten miles. The Dragon Track might be called a "world-ley."

We can't go too far into Michell's philosophy; he does it too well himself. The line of dragon-sites, though, erected by different cultures throughout Europe across thousands of years would seem to be a statement.

IV. The Message Behind the Pattern

Buffalo astronomer, artist, and mystic Franklin LaVoie is a pioneer of the sacred landscape of his native Western Door. Franklin knew of the prominent Iroquois dragon tales about the region, and for a long time had been trying to catch their meaning. He noted the world-wide identification of the Falls as a source of geomantic power. He observed the work of John Michell, and thought of taking the dragon-line around the globe. He was astonished by what he found.

On his first attempts at plotting the Old World "Dragon Track," Franklin saw that it seemed to go through Western New York in a south-westerly direction. This "St. Michael-Apollo Axis" curves over the top of the Atlantic, hits the American continent, and seems to pass down the St. Lawrence Seaway, cutting through the Western Door, passing apparently south of Buffalo through the Southern Tier and into Ohio. The line leaves the States near the notoriously haunted New Orleans, crosses the Gulf, and reenters the landmass in Mexico to soar between any number of geomantic hotspots (between ancient Mexican capitols Teotihuacan and Tenochtitlan). From there it begins again its ocean journey.

A line going northwestward through Europe might not seem aimed at Western New York on first impression, but most of the maps we look at are flat. Our globes are spherical. Franklin's diagrams seemed to make sense. Yet Franklin is a mystic; his insights are probably more reliable than those of most people, but he relies on them more. The writer of this book is not one of those who, after the resurrection of their Savior, would have believed though they did not see. Making sure of the specifics of the Dragon Track on the actual earth (as opposed to a model of it) is not an easy thing to do, and subsequent study by Franklin has neither author nor mystic convinced the work is done yet.

But Franklin returns to his original observation, the one that had put him onto this from the beginning: that there are significant dragon sites and Native American legends about the Western Door, and that the Dragon Track (when his full understanding of it is out) truly passes its mighty influence through the heart of New York's western counties.

Franklin has much more to say. He senses that the Dragon Path may be more astronomical in function than either geographical or geomantic. We urge him to get his ideas fully into writing, as we urge anyone to hear him talk. Vital questions remain.

V. IN THE PATH OF THE DRAGON

What other evidence is there that the Dragon Path has some significance for Western New York? For one thing, within its apparent course (if it is envisioned as even a few dozen miles across) lie many of the metaphysical wonders we have discussed throughout this book. "The Spirit Way" - the thirty-mile-wide band of religious activity in the Western Door - also seems to slant to the southwest, virtually within the Dragon line in Franklin's original model. Other such sites seem to lie in the same track: the serpent and alligator mounds in Ohio, and beyond it Cahokian sites in the midwest. (Even the Ohio sacred pathway might be running in the same direction.)

If any of this were true, what would be the signs, according to all we suspect about the mystical, the paranormal, and the ancient lore of the earth? What would it mean to be "in the path of the Dragon," in a region in which the Dragon Path neared a place - Niagara Falls - where human and natural energy rise together? There might be signs.

The effects would be subtle, and only evident in mass patterns. Human reactions might be quirky and paradoxical.

There would be a heightened energy affecting the religious impulse, inclining people simply to express it - good, bad, indifferent, chaotic, orthodox, irrational. Cults and communities would thrive.

There would be a high number of allegedly haunted sites. Supernatural lore of all types - classical and high-tech - would cluster.

The ancient people of the region, far more entuned than the modern, would display in their deepest myths and traditions the influence, possibly even the images, of the Dragon Track.

Let the reader be the judge.

VI. CONCLUSION

Life in the modern developed world virtually compels a form of emotional rootlessness. Most of us move about so much, separated from our places of birth, our extended families, even the natural environment. As literacy diminishes and deep exposure to the preservers of culture - myth, religion, folklore, old literature - becomes rare, the vivid, archetypal images that, circulating in each individual consciousness, used to keep us connected to something bigger and more lasting than ourselves have been largely jettisoned from everyday life. Their replacements - often random images from the mass media - don't seem up to the job, and as the twentieth century closes, it seems hard to deny that many citizens of the Western countries, particularly Americans, sense something serious missing.

For many this state of lack becomes a keen emotional hunger, a discontent with themselves, their lives, and their place. Glamor must lie elsewhere, and the dress, music, and political fashions of the day seem part of the passage to it. Some who have come to recognize it as a "spiritual" gulf that needs filling seem almost as trendy in that regard, turning in many successive directions for guidance as if the answer to all life's questions might be held by another who can quickly impart it. The answer may not be the same for all of us. It may be within us, or around us wherever we are; it may already be behind us, back where we were born, maybe in the past, well before that. For many, it may be hard to recover.

I've never heard a Native American (flocked by Whites seeking tribal mysteries) display the testiness I think I might in those shoes. "You took our land, our way of life, our freedom, and now you want... *what?*" The Native Americans, like many other people who have preserved their "connectedness" to their ancestral pasts, have often been willing to help, but some were puzzled. "Why don't you study your own ancestors?" one asked. Ah, it can all be lost in a generation or so. Those of us whose for-bears forfeited their own mysticism for the left-brain precision of technological world-beating probably don't deserve easy solutions, and they're probably impossible anyway. For resolution of the most passionate issues - for a sense of real belonging - maybe it's into each personal past and place that each individual should be looking.

It could be that, when the eternal powers authentically manifest to us, they come clothed in the archetypes of our own ancestral pasts. Maybe that explains why, in my runs in the woods, in an owl call, I think I hear a word, maybe my own name... when, on skis in an unfamiliar wood, as day congeals, and I *think* this is the trail curving back, the beat of big sudden wings thunders the branch-ends exactly timed to a prophetic thought... the shape that seemed to move just out of focus at the eye-corners, but now resembles a stump or pattern of shadow, seemed, not the Native American shaman in the region's historic past, but the cowled figure of one of the bards, skalds, or druids from my own ancestral imagination, that may never have set foot upon these lands. But there was wonder here.

This book may have been an attempt to resolve my own bemuse-ment with the Western New York area, to call out a rightful sense of wonder - to its creeks, its ridges and varied landscapes, its old churches and Masonic halls, the foundations of its cities' streets - that surely deserves to be felt, that flows up from its very roots. It may have been moved by the need to record, preserve, and pass on for another generation or two the supernatural folklore that's lasted into this. It's part of our character, and none of us know what those in future years would treasure, if it were only saved for them, from our own. Maybe my own interest in the paranormal is a bit of a protest against the habit so many have of judging without thinking, on either side of that question or any other; that practice defies what could be our better selves. But the heart of it all may be the sense that not too many people notice how influenced we all are by the past, by our own past, by our place; how we feel it when our connection to past or place is lost, how we should know it for what it is - and what a worthy place we have here.

Maybe there is some energy here that will fill many with inspiration and stubborn pride, yet keep itself forever understated, and state itself in no practical way. Maybe the kick will always go just wide (and maybe not, for all things are in cycles); but those who will ever know truly who they are will know it - once they've looked well - wherever they are, and the learning gained here can be of the true and inner kind that success alone - and its escort glamor - might never bring.

THE ST. MICHAEL-APOLLO AXIS
(from *Twelve-tribe Nations* by John Michell and Christine Rhone)

1 Skellig Michael
2 St. Michael's Mount
3 Mont St.-Michel
4 Bourges

8 Mont Sant'Angelo,
Monte Garga
9 Kerkyras
10 Delphi

5 Sagra di San Michele
6 San Michele at Castiglione
di Garfagnana
7 Perugia

11 Athens
12 Delos
13 Lindos
14 Mount Carmel

SOURCES

We wanted to make a book without either footnotes that weary
the reader or a bibliography that makes its author look smart. Our
interest in the paranormal and in history in general is longstanding, and we
sincerely cannot remember all the books that have gone into this one.

We've given credit in the text when specific information was drawn from just one source. When a subject was well-known - like Red Jacket or Thomas Lake Harris - and our contentions were not contentious, we seldom bothered to tribute a single source.

In almost no case in this book was our goal to seal the discussion of any subject. (It's pretty hard to settle anything in two pages.) We wanted to have an understanding of the issues, but our main point was usually just to call public attention to the matters of discussion.

Some of our interviewees did not want to be mentioned. We used their testimony only if we felt they believed it. Our intent was not to draw things out of people against their better selves, and in many cases we've withheld information if it might subject individuals to stress or ridicule. The book has not suffered for it.

BURIED SECRETS

Almost any old history of Western New York's counties and towns contains something interesting from the perspective of this chapter, and usually in the first fifty pages. There are a raft of books out about ancient Old World exploration of the Americas; those of Barry Fell make a good start. In our observations of the Iroquois we were helped (in this chapter and others) by two old texts, Harriet Converse' *Myths and Legends of the New York Iroquois* and *Legends of the Iroquois* by W. W. Canfield. Historic anomalies are hot commodities in the paranormal business, and Francis Hitching's *World Atlas of Mysteries* is a fine place to begin one's exposure to this subject. Additional help:

BLUFF POINT - *Thirty-fifth Annual Report of the New York State Museum of Natural History*
THE ALLEGANY SLAUGHTER-STONE - Allegany State Park historians and an article by Lucille Taylor (*Salamanca Republican-Press*)
THE CHAUTAUQUA VIKINGS - the unpublished papers of skeptical historian-farmer Norman Carlson
THE GENESEE TRADE-TOKEN - Don Eckler's letter, photograph, and the accompanying article in the *Epigraphical Society's Occasional Publications*
MYSTERY OF THE MOORING STONES - John J. Olson's article in ESOP (the *Epigraphical Society's Occasional Publications*)

PLACES OF POWER

Interviews were helpful for lore on local "Supernatural-natural" sites, but many in Western New York are nationally prominent. We got info from a number of books, including: Rosemary Ellen Guiley's *Atlas of the Mysterious in North America*, Janet and Colin Bord's *Unexplained Mysteries of the 20th Century*, and Jenny Randles' *Strange & Unexplained Mysteries of the 20th Century* and *UFOs & How to See Them*. Books by Francis Hitching (*The World Atlas of Mysteries*) and Colin Wilson (*The Mammoth Book of the Supernatural*) are good places to begin the study of earth mysteries, as well as of oddities in most categories. Extra help from:

M. I. B.'S AND UFOS - Norman Carlson's papers
MYSTERY MONSTERS - Thomas S. Cook's 1981 article (*Nunda News*); the Genesee County History Department; Norman Carlson's papers; and *Legends of New York State* by Catherine Harris Ainsworth
SECRET SERPENTS - the books of Charles Fort; a 1984 article by Bruce Westerdahl (*Rochester Democrat and Chronicle*)
THE BYRON EARTH WHEELS - the Genesee County History Department
ROCKY RAIN - from the *Rochester Democrat and Chronicle*, December 9, 1979
SPOOK HILL - an article by Katherine Seelye (August 3, 1976) in the *Rochester Democrat and Chronicle*
PITTSFORD'S MYSTERIOUS TUNNELS - the book of Shirley Cox Husted (*Valley of the Ghosts*) and interviews with Pittsford Town Historian Audrey Johnson (who quibbles with some of the hauntings)
NIAGARA FALLS - Mike Vogel's *Buffalo News* article of August 1987.

TEN CLASSIC SPOOKS

Literary sources for this chapter and the one following overlapped quite a bit. Slater Brown's *The Heyday of Spiritualism* was invaluable for both. Specific information for "Ten Classic Spooks" came from newspaper and magazine articles, and interviews with historians and historical societies. We recommend Carl Carmer and Arch Merrill, two gentlemen not exactly preoccupied with the supernatural, but who never shied away from it. Additional help:

FORT NIAGARA - interviews with historian Dennis Farmer; Eric Stutz' article in the *Niagara Gazette* (October 29, 1978); and Brian Leigh Dunnigan's 1989 article from *New York Folklore*
CASPER MEETS RONALD MCDONALD - Eric Stutz' article in the *Niagara Gazette* (October 29, 1978)
THE OCTAGON HOUSE - Shirley Cox Husted's *Valley of the Ghosts*
THE OLD MAIN STREET CEMETERY - Frank J. Lankes' books on the Ebenezer Society
HILL OF THE HELLHOUNDS - the Wales Historical Society
FOREVER ON A FALL AFTERNOON - Ben Fanton's *Buffalo News* article of February 6, 1986
THE WHITE LADY OF IRONDEQUOIT - Husted's *Valley of the Ghosts*
GREEN ACRES - the papers of the mansion's caretakers; Bill Nelson's Halloween 1970 article in the *Union Sun and Journal*.

THE SPIRIT WAY

Carl Carmer's *Listen for a Lonesome Drum* put us onto the idea of the Spirit Way and a lot else. For appreciations of nineteenth-century religious fervor in Western New York and in general, we were assisted by Michael Barkun's *Crucible of the Millennium*, Whitney R. Cross' *The Burned-over District*, and Peter Washington's wry *Madame Blavatsky's Baboon*. Books that helped us to an appreciation of the Spiritualism of the last century include Slater Brown's *The Heyday of Spiritualism*, Derek Jarrett's *The Sleep of Reason*, and R. Lawrence Moore's *In Search of White Crows*. E. W. Vanderhoof's Historical *Sketches of Western New York* present a look askance at most mystical personalities. Most old county histories contain renditions of the pertinent spiritual activity that went on within them. Other sources:

NOAH AND THE NEW JERUSALEM - *Centennial History of Erie County, New York* (Crisfield Johnson)
THE STONE OF HELP - Frank J. Lankes' books on the Ebenezers
HARMONIA - Daune Miller Palmer's article in the *Chautauqua County Mirror*
THE BROTHERHOOD OF THE NEW LIFE - Catherine McAllister's *Chautauqua County Mirror* article
THE LACKAWANNA SAINT - Buffalo State College folklorist Lydia Fish's article in the *New York Folklore Quarterly*.

THE STORYTELLER'S BAG

We're indebted to Paul Gromosiak, an authority on the Six Nations' history and a passionate advocate for their causes, for help with this chapter. Most of our observations about Cornplanter, Red Jacket, and the Iroquois come from a variety of historical texts, including books by Harriet Converse, John Niles Hubbard, W. W. Canfield, and Arthur C. Parker. Some of the classic lore comes to us in the words of Jesse Cornplanter and Cephas Hill (through the book of Carl Carmer, *Listen for a Lonesome Drum*), and from Jesse Cornplanter's own *Legends of the Longhouse*. For more recent Iroquois lore we thank the tales of Duce Bowen (*One More Story*) and Leo Cooper (*Seneca Indian Stories*). Other help:

CORNPLANTER'S ACCUSATION - Norman Carlson's papers
THE STONE GIANTS, THE OWL CAP, THE LITTLE PEOPLE, THE VAMPIRE-HERMIT, TWO FRIENDS AND THE DEVIL - For these traditional Iroquois stories we thank Jesse Cornplanter's *Tales of the Longhouse*
SOME IROQUOIS BEASTIES - Duce Bowen (*One More Story*); Ben Fanton's article in the *Buffalo News Magazine* (February 14, 1993).

TRACK OF THE ILLUMINOIDS

There are centuries of speculation about the secret societies, and a legion of books ranging from the sober (J. M. Roberts, *The Mythology of the Secret Societies*, and Peter Partner, *The Murdered Magicians*) to the delirious (quite a few). You have to listen to them all, though. *The Secret Destiny of America* (by Manly P. Hall) and *The Illuminoids* (by Neal Wilgus) were especially helpful with early American issues. For general observations of occult activity and development, we enjoyed Michael Howard's *The Occult Conspiracy*, Trevor Ravenscroft's *The Spear of Destiny*, Christopher Knight and Robert Lomas' *The Hiram Key*, and any book by Michael Baigent, Richard Leigh, and/or Henry Lincoln (but especially *Holy Blood, Holy Grail*). We can't back all their conclusions, but their spadework is helpful. Other assistance:

BUFFALO'S MYSTICAL LAYOUT - Steve Nelson's article "Washington, DC Sacred Geometry"; Dr. G Hunter Bartlett's *Andrew and Joseph Ellicott*.
THE MOHAWK MASON - *Joseph Brant: Mohawk Chief* (Jonathan Bolton and Claire Wilson)
WILLIAM MORGAN AND THE ANTIMASONIC FURY - *The Antimasonic Party* (William P. Vaughan)
THE GRAVE OF JACK THE RIPPER - Colin Wilson and Robin Odell's *Jack the Ripper: Summing up and Verdict*, and Philip Sugden's *The Complete History of Jack the Ripper*.

THE SUPERNATURAL ROYCROFT

Many of the above books contributed occult interpretations of matters Roycroft, whose roots extend widely. A. T. Mann's *Sacred Architecture*, John Michell's *The Dimensions of Paradise*, and Nigel Pennick's *Sacred Geometry* provided valuable insights into Roycroft symbolism and architecture. Bruce A. White's *The Philistine: A Periodical of Protest* was quite useful for many Roycroft basics, as was *Art & Glory*, Freeman Champney's biography of Elbert Hubbard, and *Head, Heart, and Hand*, the lovely book edited by Marie Via and Marjorie B. Searl.

We thank the Roycroft Shops and the Turgeon-Rust Gallery for our Roycroft photographs and illustrations. We thank Roycroft historian Robert Charles Rust for overseeing this chapter. Other assistance:

THE ROYCROFT SEAL - an article in the *East Aurora Advertiser* of May 13, 1948; *The Alchemist's Handbook* by "Frater Albertus."
MAGNA MATER - Rosemary Alicia Brown's *Katherine Emma Maltwood, Artist 1878-1961*

TEN MODERN SPOOKS

Most of the information for this chapter came from interviews, newspaper and magazine articles, and national compendiums of the occult (which just happen to feature some Western Door hangouts). We must include Leslie Shepard's *Encyclopedia of Occultism & Parapsychology*, Dennis William Hauck's *Haunted Places: The National Directory*, and Rosemary Ellen Guiley's *Encyclopedia of Mystical & Paranormal Experience* (fine summaries of almost anything supernatural). Louis C. Jones' *Things*

That Go Bump in the Night was also helpful with upstate folklore. Other assistance:

THE STRANGE CASE OF SASSAFRAS CHARLEY - Sidney L. Harring's January 1992 article in *New York History* magazine
FREDONIA'S IGOE HALL - Chris Shanne's *The Leader* article, October 30, 1995
THE VANISHING HITCHHIKER REVISITED - the book of Catherine Harris Ainsworth; articles by Leslie N. Ford (*Buffalo Courier-Express*, 1937) and Eric Stutz (*Niagara Gazette*, 10/29/78).
WAIF BETWEEN WORLDS - Ralph Dibble's *Buffalo Evening News* Article of January 28, 1974

THE DRAGON PATH

John Michell's *The View Over Atlantis* may be where the popular reawakening to "earth mysteries" begins. We also thank the unpublished papers of "The Dragon Project," a late-1970's "earth mysteries" study of old monuments and churches in the British Isles.

CREDITS

We thank the following - not all believers - who may not have been credited elsewhere and who helped with our research:

J.P. Allan	Carol Hody	Joe Pannullo
Donata Ahern	Jennifer Johnson	Will Parsons
"August"	Virginia Gibbs	Janet Pfohl
Mike Baister	Adam Kallif	Karen Prince
Ray Barber	Sabrina Kane	Jack Quinan
George Besch	Rob Kane	Jodee Reeland
Dennis Biglow	Jerry Kegler	Richard Riesem
Craig Braack	Grace Kirk	Ron Robertson
Mike Brown	Al Kurek	Dorothy Rolling
Pat Brown	Kenneth Kysor	Dorothy Rossell
Bruce Budney	Amy Lafferty	John and Sue Rossell
Scott Carnes	Melvin Levy	Pat Schaap
Brian Cavanagh	Jim Link	Kelly Schutrum
Quinn Caya	Vince Martonis	Ron Schwartz
Joe Citro	Johanna Mabee	Sandra Scofield
Bruce Coleman	Kim McDougall	Marjorie Searl
Sue Conklin	"Moon" McGregor	Sharon Stanley
John Creamer	Rick Miller	Tom Stouffer
"Doc" Davenport	Twylah Nitsch	Edythe Turgeon
Ernie Dellas	Dr. Joe Panebianco	Carolyn Vacca
Frances Dumas	Marjorie Perez	Jeffrey Valence
Mark Erhardt	Ron Pfeffer	Marie Via

Special mention:
The "Supernatural Roycroft" research group:
Noel Baker, Tom Bojanowski, Peter Cimino, Rose Czerny, Kathy Frost, Betsy Good, and honorary lifetime member *Jim Williams...*

And especially the noble cast of the *Erie County Historical Society Library*, unfailing in their bounty, unflagging in their spirits, and unimpressed with this dedication.

Front Cover:
Drawing: *Sue Quinby*
Architectural images: *Martha Mathewson*
Color: *Tom Bojanowski*

Extra Thanks:
Thanks to *Petit Printing Corp., Judy Kovacik , JoAnn Daehn,* and *Brian Hartmann* for putting in all the final finishing touches.

And finally, to the artists, without whom this would not have been the same book. Your reward will come, my friends.

Photo by Tom Bojanowski

MASON WINFIELD

Teacher, speaker and writer Mason Winfield studied English and classics at Denison University and earned a master's degree in British literature at Boston College. For thirteen years he taught at the Gow School (South Wales, NY), an independent boarding school for dyslexic boys. While at Gow he served as English Department chairman, was ranked several times among the Buffalo area's top ten tennis players, and won a 50K cross-country ski marathon. His interests include history, mythology, and the paranormal (with a special fondness for Celtic lore and literature). He has deep convictions about education, and may have some words on that score somewhere down the road. He plans more projects aimed at presenting the insights of the past to the present, and presenting a living world with the possibility that there might be another level to it all.

THE BIRTH OF A BUFFALO PUBLISHING FIRM

Western New York's most innovative publishing company will celebrate its 15th anniversary in 1999 by hitting a benchmark that most regional publishing houses only dream about.

Photo by Matthew Pitts

By the time the candles on the birthday cake are blown out, Western New York Wares Inc. will have moved 108,000 books and games into homes, schools and libraries across the nation. Not bad for a company that sprouted its roots in trivial turf!

The year was 1984 and the trivia craze was taking the nation by storm. As Buffalo journalist Brian Meyer played "the other trivia game" with friends in his North Buffalo living room, he came up with the notion of creating a local game that tested players' knowledge about the people, places and events in their hometown.

Western New York Trivia Quotient hit store shelves several months later, selling out is first edition in only six weeks. The newest edition is still available.

A year later, Meyer complied a book of quotations that chronicled the feisty reign of Mayor Jimmy Griffin. A follow-up volume was published eight years later to coincide with Griffin's last year in office.

Meyer, a business reporter at the *Buffalo News*, spent nearly 16 years at WBEN Radio where he served as managing editor. During his tenure, he won more state and regional awards than any other radio reporter in Western New York. Meyer covered presidential conventions and inaugurations, hurricane aftermaths in Florida and key portions of the O.J. Simpson trial in Los Angeles.

But as founder and president of Western New York Wares Inc., Meyer was also methodically building his innovative publishing company. He began collaborating with local authors, artists and photographers on a variety of book projects, all of them with a regional flavor.

By 1998, the region's premier publisher of local books and games had more than 45 products in its catalog.

Meyer is a graduate of the Marquette University College of Journalism, St. Joseph's Collegiate Institute and Buffalo Public School #56. He teaches communications courses at a number of local institutions, including Buffalo State College and Medaille College. A movie buff, Meyer also enjoys spending summer weekends hiking and canoeing at his cottage at Rushford Lake in Allegany County.

OTHER BOOKS DISTRIBUTED BY WESTERN NEW YORK WARES

The Ghosthunter's Journal: Supernatural Tales From Upstate New York - Mason Winfield takes readers on spellbinding fictional journeys that have been penned based on his factual research of the region's supernatural legacy. The riveting book will be released September 15, 1999.
ISBN: *1-879201-29-1* $10.95

Western New York Weather Guide - Readers won't want any "winteruptions" as they breeze through this lively book which focuses on Buffalo's four seasons. Penned by Channel 7 weather guru Tom Jolls with assistance from Brian Meyer and Joseph Van Meer, this first-of-a-kind guide focuses on humorous, dramatic and historic weather events over the past century.
ISBN: *1-879201-18-1* $7.95

A View Through the Lens of Robert L. Smith: Buffalo Bills Photos - Bills owner Ralph Wilson says the 444 photos in this unique collection "provide enjoyment and touches of nostalgia I wouldn't trade for a first round draft choice." This eye-grabbing photographic journey chronicles the team's ups and downs from its inception in 1960 to the end of the Jim Kelly era.
ISBN: *1-879201-17-8* $26.95

Beyond Buffalo: A Photographic Journey and Guide to the Secret Natural Wonders of our Region - Full-color photographs and informative vignettes showcase 30 remarkable sites in Western New York. Author David Lawrence Reade includes complete directions and tips for enjoying each site.
ISBN: *1-879201-19-4* $19.95

Exploring Niagara: The Complete Guide to Niagara Falls and Vicinity - Filled with 77 spectacular full color photos, the guide includes dozens of tours of wineries, canals, waterfalls, mansions and forests. Authors Hans and Allyson Tammemagi also chronicle the history which has shaped our region.
ISBN: *0-9681815-0-3* $14.25

Look Who's Adopted! - This unique book is written for children who are adopted. Penned by local attorney Michael Taheri, the father of two adopted children, this beautifully illustrated book encourages kids to peer into their exciting futures.
ISBN: *1-879201-21-6* $8.95

Buffalos Treasures: A Downtown Walking Guide - Readers are led on a fascinating tour of 25 major buildings. A user-friendly map and dozens of photos and illustrations supplement a text written by Jan Sheridan.
ISBN: *1-879201-15-1* $4.95

Church Tales of the Niagara Frontier: Legends, History & Architecture - This first-of-a-kind book traces the rich history and folklore of the region through accounts of 60 area churches and places of worship. Written by Austin M. Fox and illustrated by Lawrence McIntyre
ISBN: *1-879201-13-5* $14.95

Water Over the Falls: 101 of the Most Memorable Events at Niagara Falls - Daredevils who defied the Mighty Niagara, tragic rock slides and heroic rescues. More than 100 true-to-life tales are vividly recounted by noted local historian Paul Gromosiak.
ISBN: *1-879201-16-X* $5.95

Niagara Falls Q & A: Answers to the 100 Most Common Questions About Niagara Falls - Author Paul Gromosiak spent four summers chatting with 40,000 Falls tourists. This invaluable guide answers the most commonly asked questions.
ISBN: *0-9620314-8-8* $4.50

Zany Niagara: The Funny Things People Say About Niagara Falls - A fun-filled tour of humorous happenings and historical oddities. Penned by Paul Gromosiak and illustrated by John Hardiman.
ISBN: *1-879201-06-2* $4.95

Soaring Gulls & Bowing Trees: The History of the Islands Above Niagara Falls - The magnetism and history of Niagara Falls spring to life in this insightful book by Paul Gromosiak.
ISBN: *0-9620314-6-1* $9.95

Designated Landmarks of the Niagara Frontier - a riveting look at the region's architectural past. About 100 landmarks spring to life in a book written by Austin Fox and illustrated by Lawrence McIntyre.
ISBN: *0-9620314-2-9* $13.95

Symbol & Show: The Pan-American Exposition of 1901 - An insightful look at perhaps the greatest event in Buffalo history. The 128-page book was written by Austin Fox and illustrated by Lawrence McIntyre.
ISBN: *0-6816410-4-5* $13.95

Rescue of a Landmark: Frank Lloyd Wright's Darwin D. Martin House - The untold story of the abandonment and rescue of Western New York's most architecturally significant home is recounted by art historian Marjorie L. Quinlan.
ISBN: *0-9620314-7-X* $9.95

Buffalo's Waterfront: A Guidebook - Edited by Tim Tielman, this 72-page guide showcases more than 100 shoreline sites. The work includes a special fold-out map. Published by the Preservation Coalition of Erie County.
ISBN: *1-879201-00-3* $5.95

The World According to Griffin: The End of an Era - Compiled by veteran broadcast journalist Brian Meyer, this almanac includes hundreds of "Griffinisms" from one of the most feisty mayors in Buffalo history.
ISBN: *1-879201-11-9* $5.95

The A-to-Z Bus Tour of Buffalo (and Beyond) - This coloring book takes young-sters on an exciting alphabetical tour of Western New York. Seven-year-old Christin Ratzel co-authored the book with Brian Meyer. Grand Island artist Anna Finkel illustrated it.
ISBN: *1-879201-10-0* $3.50

The Cheap Gourmets' Dining Guide - Familiar veterans of local suppertime struggles, Polly and Doug Smith dish out a lively 96-page dining guide.
ISBN: *1-879201-07-0* $5.95

Buffalo City Hall: Americanesque Masterpiece - Local Historian John Conlin has penned this authoritative guide which chronicles the history and architectural significance of this regional icon.
ISBN: *1-879201-14-3* $5.95

Buffalo Chips: The Book - More than 100 rib-tickling entrees from local cartoonist Tom Stratton.
ISBN: *0-9620314-3-7* $4.95

Kid's First: A First Aid Guide For Kids - An educational book for youngsters from age 5 to 10 and their families. Authored by registered nurses Beth Kent-Astrella and Angie Leonard and illustrated by Carol Kent Williams, the book provides basic first aid information.
ISBN: *1-879201-12-7* $4.50

Quotable Cuomo: The Mario Years - An offbeat almanac of political quotes and anecdotes compiled by Mary Murray and Brian Meyer.
ISBN: *1-879201-03-8* $5.95

Hometown Heroes: Western New Yorkers in Desert Storm - (Brian Meyer and Tom Connolly)
ISBN: *1-879201-04-6* $5.95

Buffalo: A Bulls Eye View - An offbeat almanac of local anecdotes.
ISBN: *0-6816410-5-3* $4.95

Buffalo Bluff - a game of cunning hometown deception.
ISBN: *0-9620314-5-3* $6.95

Western New York Trivia Quotient - More than 1,300 trivia questions make for a fast-paced game.
ISBN: *0-9620314-0-2* $6.95

ALSO: write to us for information about our customized Buffalo Baskets!

Please include 8% sales tax and $2 for shipping. Or write for a catalog of all regional books and games:

Western New York Wares Inc.
Attention: Brian Meyer
P.O. Box 733, Ellicott Station
Buffalo, New York 14205

Internet Site Focuses on Local History, Sports, Weather and Tourist Attractions

Our unique web site is a treasure trove of information for those who enjoy learning about the people, places and events that have shaped Western New York.

The site showcases full-color photography from some of the region's most respected shutterbugs and literary passages from many best-selling regional books. The works of more than 30 local authors, photographers and game inventors are included.

Browsers will enjoy meandering through the many "departments" of our cyberspace bookstore:

Ghosts: East Aurora author Mason Winfield shares some "ghostly" insights into paranormal happenings in Western New York.

Weather: Channel 7 weather guru Tom Jolls chronicles many of the most memorable, humorous and dramatic tales about Buffalo's four seasons.

Sports: Buffalo Bills photographs spring to life, courtesy of respected photographer Robert L. Smith.

The internet site also includes sections on nature, Niagara Falls, architecture and food. There's even a special department for kids!

www.wnybooks.com